Rhythmic Reflections On Creative Teaching

Jon Hazilla

Mosaic Eye Publishing, Brookline, MA
mosaiceyepublishing.com

Copyright © 2013 by Jon Hazilla

Cover design by Victoria Arico

All rights reserved. This book contains material protected under International and Federal Copyright Laws and Treaties. Any unauthorized reprint or use of this material is prohibited. No part of this book may be reproduced or transmitted in any form or by any means, electronic or mechanical, including photocopying, recording, or by any information storage and retrieval system without express written permission from the author.

ISBN 978-0-578-12722-4

First Edition

Printed in the United States of America

In memory and dedication to my brother,
whose birthday I share, a perfect decade apart...

Dr. Michael Hazilla
July 15, 1946 – October 21, 2010

"spirit not to lose..."

Acknowledgements

A heartfelt thank you and love to the many people involved in the evolution and transformation of my manuscript...Louise Grant, Roger Brown, Gerry Leader, Dr. John Jones, Chungliang Al Huang, Camille Colatosti, Rebecca Cline, Steve Wilkes, Forrest Hodgkins, John Ramsay, Tom Regis, Dr. Suzanne Hanser, Ellie Boynton, Melissa Howe, Sue Elinsky, Sunny-san, Skip Hadden, Dave DiCenso, Jerry Kalaf, Bill Laughlin, Bronwyn Jones, Jonathan Feist, Debbie Cavalier, Maryann Tamagni, Z.M.M., and my four sisters, Irene, Maria, Paulette, and Barbara.

Continued thank you(s) to all who I've undoubtedly missed (please forgive me) and have helped in big and small ways... And special acknowledgement to my students who continue to inspire me, and without them this book would not exist...

And finally, with deep gratitude to my editor, William Dean, who masterfully rearranged my thoughts into cohesive sentences. My "Reflections" would not have made it to print, without his brilliant mind, and flowing command of the English language...much love William.

Table of Contents

INTRODUCTION	xv
RHYTHMIC REFLECTIONS	1
HONESTY	7
MOTIVATION	13
VALIDATION	19
GRADES	23
KNOWLEDGE	31
ROLE MODEL	39
COMMUNICATION	47
FRIENDSHIP	59
TECHNIQUES FOR CREATIVE TEACHING	65
"ZEN THOUGHTS FROM MY TEACHING"	77
CELL PHONE and iPOD GENERATION	81
MUSIC AS THERAPY	89
MENTORS	97
Mosaic	103
Bibliography	104

"Show up...

    pay attention...

        tell the truth...

            don't be attached to results..."

~ Angeles Arrien, Anthropologist
4 rules for living

Two monks were arguing over a philosophical question as their teacher passed by. They stopped him and asked him to settle their disagreement. The first monk explained his understanding, to which the teacher replied, "You're right." The second monk protested, and made his argument, which was the complete opposite of what the first monk had said. The teacher then answered the second monk, saying, "You're right." A third monk who had been listening asked in frustration, "But Master, you tell both of these monks that they are right, when their explanations are contradictory and couldn't possibly both be correct." The teacher replied, "You're right!"

~ Zen Story

"Teachers open the door,

but you must enter by yourself..."

~ Chinese Proverb

INTRODUCTION

Emerson said that everything we learn is the result of observation. This book is based on 25 years of observations I have made while teaching at Berklee College and New England Conservatory in Boston, Massachusetts. During my time as a teacher I have had many conversations with individuals involved in the education process, and those discussions have informed my writing. Nevertheless, this book is not intended to be a broad representation of teaching methods at a host of different institutions. For argument's sake, I consider Berklee to be a typical liberal arts college that excels and distinguishes itself in all styles of contemporary music.

I believe that teachers at all academic levels can benefit from reading these observations and the ideas they've inspired, and it is my hope that I can say something meaningful not just to educators but to other mentors, protégés, and even non-teachers. The more precise we are in defining and targeting our educational objectives, the easier it will be to accomplish those objectives. The archer has a greater chance of hitting the bull's-eye when it is only the bull's-eye that he sees. The archer becomes a better archer by missing the bull's-eye 99 times and hitting it on the 100th attempt... so too with education; it may be an imperfect art, but concentration and practice cannot fail to strengthen its aim.

In my 25 years of observation and teaching I have encountered many recurring themes. *Honesty*, *Motivation*, *Knowledge*, *Communication*, and *Role Model* – each one a chapter in this book – are themes one will encounter and reflect on innumerable times in a teaching career. *Honesty* is a virtue that should shadow all of what we do in life. As a teacher, it should be a magnified extension of one's own life. There is a distinction between *Motivation* and inspiration. Both require strong guidance, but we cannot be responsible for motivating our students... we can only inspire them to follow the paths we have paved. *Knowledge* is an accumulation of life experience. Teaching is a concentrated form of experience that reflects our expertise. How we *Communicate* and impart the knowledge we have acquired will be the difference between a "success-filled" education and one that is "less-filled." Some of our biggest influences in life were our teachers. They were in fact our greatest *Role Models*, or as the late great U.C.L.A. coach John Wooden reminds us, "Being a role model is the most powerful form of education."

Other themes that are equally important but perhaps encountered less often in a teaching career are *Friendship* and *Validation*. *Friendship* is an extension of *Role Model* but we must be wary of its natural evolution in teaching; we should clearly define the boundaries of a student-teacher friendship so nothing inhibits the education process. *Validation* is a critical component that must be present for our students to develop a sense of trust in what we teach. *Grades* and the entire grading process are unique to teaching, and the process is forever evolving. But one must maintain a constant vigilance to remain fair and objective. *Creative Techniques* and *Zen Thoughts From My Teaching* are experiential and reflect the evolution of my teaching philosophy and style. Upon further contemplation and my ongoing involvement in the Music Therapy Department at Berklee, it was obvious to me that I should include a chapter devoted to *Music As Therapy*. The continuing research and omnipresence of music in all cultures throughout the world strongly supports music as a viable therapy and validates its long overdue acceptance as a form of healing.

As my manuscript has evolved over two and a half decades it has become apparent that the proliferation of cell phones and iPods inside and outside the classroom must be addressed. *The Cell Phone and iPod Generation* may influence

INTRODUCTION

and alter *how* we teach but it will never change the recipe for success-filled teaching. In conclusion, my book would not be complete (or even exist at all) without the ongoing guidance of my *Mentors* and the *Rhythmic Reflections* of my students.

Successful teaching incorporates two main ingredients. The first ingredient for successful teaching is a true love for teaching. I have a deep passion for my vocation that is carefully entwined with an even deeper caring for my students. If I am ever too harsh, it is with the intent of cultivating a blossom that will bloom beyond the present moment.

I was appalled and angry the first time a colleague remarked that he "disliked teaching" and only did it for the money. This statement may be more prevalent in a music vocation – where a steady gig to pay the bills is a rarity – but nonetheless, it is utterly unacceptable and entirely unfair to his students. The truly tragic part of a teacher's detachment from teaching, is that students easily detect this attitude. So how or why should they be encouraged to learn, seek, or improvise?

It may be a reality of my profession that musicians find it necessary to supplement their incomes by teaching, but that does not mean a musician cannot be a great ACTIVE performer and a great teacher as well. The demands are greater, but the rewards are even more satisfying. In fact, the paradox of the "music teaching profession" is, can one maintain an active performance schedule and be fully committed to teaching as well? The answer is yes and yes. I strongly believe that the two cannot exist separately in the teaching profession. One might be an outstanding performer and not a great teacher, but you cannot be an excellent teacher without performing. This is not to say that commitment and attitudes do not sway over lengthy time periods, but the teaching profession itself is nurturing and rejuvenating. Sabbaticals and summers off allow for fresh thinking every September.

Caring is the second-most important ingredient of good teaching. Milton Mayeroff in his book *On Caring* states, "In order to care I must understand the other's needs and I must be able to respond properly to them, and clearly good intentions do not guarantee this. To care for someone, I must know many things. I must know for example who the other is, what his powers and limitations are, what his needs are, and what is conducive to his growth; I must know how to respond to his needs, and what my own powers and limitations are."

The author Norman Maclean has a similar opinion and states: "A great teacher is a tough guy who cares deeply about something that is hard to understand." Moreover, I find the love of your profession and a deep caring for your students to be inseparable.

At a recent meeting the issue of published phone numbers and allowing students to have access to you at home was being debated. A few colleagues adamantly opposed the publication of their home numbers because they did not want to be contacted at home. That is their prerogative. I routinely give out my home phone number and students rarely contact me at all; never do I consider it a bother. The students who do call are the ones who need help the most, and that is what I want... I want to help students who struggle because I care about them and that's the template for a success-filled education.

Sadly, such a disconnected attitude infects all minds on many levels. Granted only a teacher with impressive credentials and a worthy resume should be considered for a teaching job, but more important than even these factors is their innate desire to teach! This should be paramount in their hiring. Great teachers inspire great students.

I do not consider my profession to be "9 to 5," and at 5:00 PM cease all contact with students. Perhaps the greatest exchange of knowledge comes after 5:00 – not within the confines of the classroom but beyond them, in the arena of friendship. It is no secret that many a professional friendship and provocative idea have germinated on the MIT campus at the Muddy River Pub. I have a very strict rule not to socialize with any student before graduation, but once they have graduated, I welcome this deeper level of friendship. It has been my past experience with

INTRODUCTION

former teachers that I always learned more from them in our ensuing friendship than in any hourly lecture or private lesson.

The strength of any institution – indeed, its very ability to survive – is based on the quality of its teachers and their ability to attract and guide motivated students. In turn, a group of high-quality graduates will encourage strong future candidates to refertilize the institute from which they have just graduated. The teacher/student relationship is sacred and a mirror image of itself. The better the teacher, the better the student. We are two strands on the same string of education. A stagnant teacher creates a lifeless educational environment.

The absolute chief criteria for any initial hiring, and for continued employment, should be a *LOVE FOR TEACHING*. Why not put greater emphasis in the interviewing process on the *reasons* a future teacher desires to teach? Don't assume anything. This should be a critical component of the interview process. A probation period of one year would serve as a reference point to demonstrate the candidate's ability to teach, as well as his or her *desire* to teach. We might receive fewer applications, but the individuals who do come forth would be there for the right reason… THE LOVE OF TEACHING. I love teaching and I love my students. We are both seekers of new knowledge. Often I say to my students that we are very similar. I may have acquired more knowledge and life experience but we are both equals. Mark Twain once flippantly said, "The art of prophecy is difficult to predict especially with regard to the future," and so I cannot be quite sure what path education will follow from this day forward. But my ideas for its course are simple and, I believe, fundamentally sound. I feel strongly that my ideas would have been just as useful 100 years ago as they are at the present moment; I have great confidence that they will prove just as important 100 years hence.

Chapter One

RHYTHMIC REFLECTIONS

*"It is a serious thing to interfere with another man's life.
It is hard enough to guide one's own."*

~ Gilbert Highet

I started studying with Jon at a time when many conflicting, ambiguous, and often too conceptual teaching methods from previous teachers had left me confused and low in confidence. Jon immediately engaged me with his objective, focused, and structured lessons. His absolute dedication to his instrument and the art of teaching is an example to anyone, but Jon's real gift is his ability to simultaneously challenge and inspire his students through his high standards and calculated encouragement. With Jon, practicing and improving my playing became addictive! This book is a fascinating insight into Jon's methods and philosophy, gained through his many years of teaching experience, providing a fascinating pedagogical model that can be applied to teaching in many fields.

Patrick Kunka
Aberdeen, Scotland

I first studied with Jon in 2006 while I was a student at Berklee College of Music and subsequently for two months in the summer of 2011. The time I spent with Jon has been the most significant periods of my musical growth. His way of teaching is the perfect balance between the two extreme schools of thought. One emphasizes technique, versus the other that deals with the more philosophical aspects of performance. Jon is an incredibly patient and pragmatic teacher who presents all his topics in a crystal-clear manner and will calmly persevere with it until it is totally imbibed by the student. His influence on my playing extends far beyond the classroom. Now, it is as if a part of my brain is dedicated to everything that I have been taught by him, and that he is a constant presence every time I sit down to practice.

Reuben Narain
New Delhi, India

Everybody knows that Jon is an amazing teacher/drummer/composer. I had the privilege to study with Jon for more than a year at Berklee. Walking into Jon's studio was like walking into a doctor's clinic. Jon would ask me to play a little bit, while he would walk around and observe me. When I was finished, he would tell me what my problems were and would suggest clear solutions for each one of them. But it was the exuberance and joy that Jon always radiated that left an indelible mark on me. As I got to know Jon and became closer to him, I realized what a spiritually evolved person he is. Studying with him was such a great experience, and he will always be a constant reminder of how to live a life full of happiness and joy!

Deepak Edakkattil Gopinath
Boston, Massachusetts

Jon Hazilla has been a friend, teacher, and mentor to me for almost 15 years. My lessons with Jon began as a 15 year-old with no jazz background and little formal education. However, from day one Jon made me feel motivated, excited, and talented. Being the avid student and practitioner that he is, Jon always made it clear that our work as musicians is never done and this is something to be grateful for. His countless hours spent teaching, practicing, performing, and running have helped shape him into the spiritually sound individual I have had the great pleasure of knowing and learning from all these years. If geographical boundaries keep you from learning directly from Jon, I'm sure this book will be a perfect substitute.

Jordan Perlson
Brooklyn, New York

    I can honestly say that the lessons I took from Jon represented a turning point in my playing. Up until that time, I had done a fair amount of studying, but I feel that a lot of it missed the point. Jon helped open my ears to the broader scope of music, thus shifting my focus from *what* was being played to *why* it was being played. I remember at our first lesson I said that I was interested in developing technique, and so we proceeded for a couple of weeks to focus on technique. Jon quickly realized however that my technique was good enough for the time being and that I didn't understand the importance of keeping a consistent pulse on the ride cymbal. We spent some time listening to Tony Williams, particularly the earlier recordings with which I was unfamiliar. The touch he had on that cymbal was amazing! Another concept Jon introduced me to and helped me with greatly was that of resolution points, as discussed in Bob Moses' book *Drum Wisdom*, which I quickly bought. This has helped me to begin to play phrases, rather than just pecking on the snare while playing time. I recall a time when Jon asked me to solo with the brushes, first using two hands on the kit and then only one. After one chorus of 32 bars he asked me, "Which one do you like better?" I preferred the one-handed version, and he agreed that I made more music when playing with only one hand. With a limitation on the speed of notes I could play, I was forced to try to find melodic ideas or ways to make the solo interesting, rather than just playing fast notes. These are just a few of my specific memories of Jon's teaching, and every one of them enriched my playing and my life.

Forest Muther
Seoul, Korea

RHYTHMIC REFLECTIONS ON CREATIVE TEACHING

Practice, practice, practice! I remember watching Jon play in our first lesson and thinking that I should just stop now. The focus, discipline, and drive that Jon had was something that I've never seen in any of my teachers. Jon helped me get through my injuries by helping me relearn about my body and myself. He pushed me to go outside myself and to really get at the core of what I was trying to learn. Any questions I had about music or drumming he had an answer that would help right away. Always going for more, the pedagogy that Jon had worked out fueled my desire to learn. I was never happy with myself and what I was capable of in front of Jon. He was unstoppable to me. If I didn't give 300 percent he would let me know. The energy that drove his passions floored me every time. I know now that I was changed by Jon's teaching. Whenever I tackle a problem on the drums, Jon is always there in my mind. Thanks to my drum father and friend.

Devin Drobka
Brooklyn, New York

From a drumming standpoint, Jon gave me the tools I needed and still use to this day. The material we worked on together gave me more than enough technique to express the musical ideas I wanted to convey, and the extended exposure to his methodology taught me that any musical problem could be broken down in a logical way and tackled in manageable chunks. After studying with him, I truly came to believe that nothing in music was difficult, but rather simply unfamiliar. On a much deeper level, Jon taught me about being in the moment. When I got to Berklee, I was so eager to excel and do well that I was always focused on results at the expense of the process. This finally manifested itself with me considering quitting Berklee and music all together, simply because I felt so inadequate in comparison to the ideal I felt I needed to be. In a way that I will never forget, Jon lovingly and patiently sat me down and helped me through it all. In our time together, the most important thing he taught me was to be focused on the

process more than the result, and that the MOST important part of it all was to enjoy the journey and the work. Today, I find that this applies to everything in my life. Jon, through the way he teaches and lives, epitomizes the ideal of being fully PRESENT from moment to moment, and that is something I aspire to every day.
Wen Ming Soh
Singapore, Malaysia

I started taking lessons from Jon because I wanted to focus on my brush technique and I was told he was the man in Boston for that. Not only was he the *"man for brushes"* having a trillion tips and exercises, he ended up becoming an extremely supportive mentor. It was such a relief having a teacher that genuinely cared about you. I was going through a time of transition when I was getting more interested in pop music rather then jazz and Jon was my only teacher that supported my evolving interest. Jon took me under his wing, and his continued guidance has transcended into a valuable and enduring friendship.
Gabe Smith
Boston, Massachusetts

I have known Jon Hazilla for about 10 years. Jon is an inspiration in many ways – his commitment to physical and spiritual fitness (running, eating well, drinking well), regular practice of his instrument (showing up before teaching every morning to warm up for an hour), and his sense of balance (carefully considered priorities, plenty of vacation, diligent preparation for whatever he commits to). Playing piano in Jon's trio was a lesson in playing for the fun of it despite his high standards, a lesson in the pursuit of rhythmic variety, and on overall wonderful growing experience for me. I feel blessed to count Jon as a dear friend, and I always benefit from the wisdom he shares every time we get together. I will treasure this collection

of his thoughts and insights into teaching, learning, and living.
Rebecca Cline
Associate Professor
Ensemble Department
Berklee College

    I use to play in a band with Jon called "*Six Drum Sets.*" Our live performances always ended with each band member striking a carefully positioned gong and then walking offstage. The blocking for this part of the concert always had Jon as the last person to exit, stage right. At one particular concert, Jon decided not to strike the gong upon exiting. Instead, he simply approached the instrument with the full intent to strike it… but instead, quietly dampened it with his right hand and then continued to walk off. It was a stunning moment: the audience sat in a prolonged expectant hush before erupting into applause. Great drummers know the value of silence.
Steve Wilkes
Professor
Percussion Department
Berklee College

Chapter Two

HONESTY

"Buy truth, and do not sell it; get wisdom and instruction and understanding..."

~ Unknown

In education, at any given moment, being honest is unequivocally the most important task at hand in broadening and shaping young minds. Whether it is an embarrassing admission of one's own mistake, or the circumspect critique of a performance, the manner in which you relate to your students can have a dramatic, permanent influence, and honesty is as important as tactfulness.

Educators' truthfulness is a priority to ensure their continued desire to seek, learn, and question. In their book *The Elements of Teaching*, James Banner and Harold Cannon give a simple directive: "Any errors in teachers' presentations discovered after the fact must be admitted and corrected as soon as possible." As educators, your honesty and willingness to admit a mistake is the first stone in the foundation of your educational house.

You must always choose and convey your words prudently. Words are necessary in communicating your ideas as educators. At times, the words you choose may be interpreted as negative, but if filled with truth and coated with honesty, the final experience will always be positive.

Speaking honest words is a very arduous and delicate

task. However well aimed, however good your intentions, your words do not always find their intended mark. I am often asked to reveal my opinion. Like many teachers, I have a reluctance to reveal my thoughts at the first temptation. It is more important to reveal your words gradually, at selected moments, when they will have their most profound impact, rather than volunteering your full opinion at the first given opportunity. This allows the students to think on their own, rather than being influenced by your opinion.

After all classroom performances (e.g., a rudimental snare drum class or trio ensemble), I ask students to critique one another before revealing my own thoughts and criticisms. I witness a remarkable transition of student critiques during the semester, from a reluctance to say anything, to a full immersion of thought and body. On a simplistic level, this activity ensures that everyone gets involved and is present in the moment. More broadly, when faced with the task of evaluating their peers, the students – whether they realize it or not – receive a lesson in ear training that sharpens their critical skills of listening and observing, a life-long lesson that should serve them well far beyond the classroom.

In David Reynolds' book *Playing Ball on Running Water* – in which Reynolds lives Morita therapy, a character-building process developed in the early 20th century in Japan – he states, "Observation helps to be aware of what reality is bringing us to do, in each moment. How can we be aware of what needs doing, when we aren't paying attention to our circumstances?"

One cannot speak honestly in the classroom, without critical observation. You must remain vigilant and constantly remind students to pay attention to the smallest details in their own practice and performance. Body posture, breathing in relation to musical phrases, and symmetry in hand position are simple beginning points for important daily self-observation and critique. If students can be acutely aware of what they are doing in their own practice and performance and the effect it has on them, they in turn will become more conscious of what they see in others. It is more important to see the blind man than for the blind man to see us.

HONESTY

Students at first are reluctant to tell the truth when asked to judge their peers. Even asking questions may be frowned upon. (This reticence may stem initially from certain cultural mores, but in fact no students are eager to openly criticize their peers.) If a performance is bad or they did not like it, they rarely acknowledge their true feelings, offering instead a generic "I liked it." Perhaps through further questioning it may become apparent that they did not like the performance, or even worse, didn't listen at all to the piece. It doesn't matter that the truth was not revealed at first. This is one small opportunity for you to question their passive and active participation, and it allows you to reveal your own opinion in small bits and pieces. You can actively steer students, by questioning every word they use, and the honesty with which they say it. More importantly, your questioning increasingly reveals to the students the importance of honesty in their words and thoughts, and encourages them to embrace truth and accept the added weight that accompanies it.

As a teacher, you will be constantly evaluating students, and may be "put on the spot" during your critiques. Sometimes it is easier to be thoroughly honest with a student one on one – in a private lesson or office hour, for example – than when his peers are circled around him in a classroom. That is not to say that you should ever be dishonest. Some of your honesty may simply be held in reserve until the class has been dismissed. It is best to comment on the performance in brief to satisfy the individual involved, reserving a more thorough analysis for a private moment. This way, you can wisely avoid unintentionally embarrassing the student in front of the class.

One time I came very close to doing just that. Berklee's class structure (private lessons, ensembles, and labs) allows students to conceivably take several hours (three to four) a week with a particular teacher. In a short period of time, a natural closeness develops. I endorse this concentrated learning approach of layering contact hours in mixed forums. One student who embraced this approach performed a very under-prepared solo. I asked the class to critique his solo. Most were polite, saying they liked it and offering nothing of substance. Then, it was my turn. The student looked at me and said, "Don't sugarcoat it!" He knew what was coming. He didn't practice the piece enough; he stopped several times during the performance, and technically what the piece demanded was beyond his means. I was particularly harsh, partly at his urging, but felt bad about it almost immediately afterwards. After class I asked him to stay and I apologized. He said it was unnecessary – that I'd been 100% right, and everything I said was true. He thanked me for the criticisms and gave me a hug!

Students will admire and respect you for being honest. I have had students leave lessons with the comment they feel like quitting… without fail, I give them a firm handshake and remind them what the great jazz drummer Joe Morello once told me: "Success is a dumb quitter." There are many positives to garner from having approached the point of giving up. I know that despite the frustrations they are feeling at that moment, my students leave inspired by the content of the encouragement I impart to them. During the ensuing lessons I am constantly rewarded as I witness the renewed focus and energy nurtured by my honesty and support.

The flip side to your reluctance to praise is that when you do commend a student, it creates a unique fulfilling moment because of your careful reserve in previous lessons. This underscores the value of honesty. Many times, after praising a student, I will look her dead in the eye and say, "You know I wouldn't just say that." Invariably, she promptly smiles back and replies, "Yeah, I know YOU!" Mission accomplished! A bond forms and a TRUST develops that will never be broken.

Several weeks into a new semester, I will ask students how many of them completed the last assignment. I put them on the spot, watching as most heads nod up and down accordingly. I will assume they are all telling the truth, and empathetically say to them that I have no reason to doubt them. I employ this tactic throughout the semester. If stressed enough, it will encourage honesty, responsibility, and hopefully a renewed determination in

HONESTY

students who may have fallen behind to fulfill future assignments. I also tell them that I can see it in their faces if they do not tell the truth. The ones who look at the floor or out the window are a dead giveaway. I subtly encourage these students to admit to me and to the class that they did not fulfill their assignment; when students are honest about their shortcomings, it promotes an air of respect – both for their peers and for me – and inevitably prompts them to be more diligent in the future. So long as this dialogue unfolds without intimidation or embarrassment, it is a win-win situation.

Sometimes in midterms or finals I will ask a student to pick some examples from the coursework that gave her the most trouble. The content of the courses that I teach covers a wide variety of drum set skills and are performance based. Once I hear her selections, I diffuse the tension of the testing atmosphere further, by explaining that some of those same examples gave me problems too. If the student plays the examples with great ease, then she has likely missed the point of telling the truth about which portions were the hardest ones for her. Unless the student, through practice, has actually perfected the technique that she once found so difficult, I generally discover that she is just afraid to tell the truth for fear it will reflect negatively upon her grade. Whether the student is forthcoming or not, testing by this method provides a valuable lesson in honesty. For the candid student this test reveals the truth about her own difficulties and allows me to better guide her development; for the dishonest student, nothing productive comes of the test itself, simply because she chose to abuse the option of telling the truth. I am hopeful that students who take this "easy way out" reflect on the decision, and consider that in truth they have hindered their own growth through dishonesty. The truth is the only acceptable option, in an academic environment. As Mark Twin observed, "when you tell the truth you never have to remember what you said."

I recently gave a final to a student and it was apparent he had put very little thought and preparation into composing his piece. This was an extension of his class work all semester – a minimal amount of time invested, coasting on his natural abilities and talent, an "A" student doing "C" work. I asked him if he spent time on the piece, and he said "very little." This was a perfect opportunity for me to share with him my observations of his work that semester. I was honest and direct. I inquired why he took the class, what were his dreams and goals, and why had he been so detached all semester? He said he specifically came to Berklee to study with one teacher and now wants to move to L.A. with his band and "make it." It took great restraint not to offer my opinion, but he didn't ask for it. It was easier for me to reflect on his story. I knew other parts of his story, and I was particularly fond of this student. We both had deep respect for one another. It was the respect that allowed each of us to be honest with each other. There were reasons for his lack of enthusiasm and preparation that I sensed. He was sincere and honest in his explanation. I was honest too. He got a "C." And I hope he asks me for my opinion about L.A. before he moves.

  The words you choose in communicating your ideas to students must at all times be prudently selected. It should never be our intent as teachers to harm or embarrass our pupils. Embarrassment can severely stunt a student's educational growth and desire to learn – it serves no purpose in an academic setting and is an enemy to all forms of education. The words you choose and how you share them will be more carefully examined in my next chapter on motivation. Never lose sight of the fact that at all times the words you share must always speak the truth.

Chapter Three

MOTIVATION

"No motivation can live where faith and courage are absent."

~ Unknown

Motivating students is one of the most difficult assignments teachers and mentors undertake. Consequently, you should tell your students that desire must come from within, and that the will to practice – to strive for greatness – must emanate from the love of doing it, and not from any other source or reason. A student must not be preoccupied with outcome or results; rather it is the process, the practice, the *doing* that is its own reward. Mozart and Beethoven did not wait to become inspired. Every day they would sit at the keyboard and compose. Inspired or not, productive or not, it was their daily ritual and self-discipline that was the reward, not the symphony several years later.

In Rainer Maria Rilke's book *Letters to a Young Poet*, Rilke encounters a young soldier with whom he has corresponded; the soldier asks whether his poetry is good or bad, and should he continue to write? Rilke responds that he cannot answer that question for him, rather he should look deep inside himself for the answers and that he should learn to "love the questions themselves."

Regardless of what level or subject you teach, you will encounter and spend a substantial amount of time with the unmotivated or semi-interested student. Even students who are motivated most of the time will encounter practice/study slumps or ruts as they go through their academic careers. All musicians experience this on a periodic basis, as their professional careers unfold, and they should embrace and reflect upon the circumstances surrounding the lull. Slumps occur for a variety of reasons, and by analyzing those reasons, you can reshape your practice habits or, if necessary, change what you are practicing. Most importantly, a rut encourages you to periodically reexamine "why" you are practicing.

As Philip Toshio Sudo says in his book *Zen Guitar*, "Practice alone does not make perfect, perfect practice makes perfect." It is important to note that doctors and lawyers always make reference to their "practice." They never arrive. Hopefully, they continue to evolve and improve by practicing. Their vocation is their practice, and their practice is their vocation. Music is no less serious, and your practice defines your music.

One time I had a new student who I was only beginning to understand and know. He was enormously talented and creative, but he had some rough edges. It became apparent as our lessons progressed that he was over-enthusiastic and wanted new information every week when he had not even comprehended the material from the previous lesson. It was apparent that he was not a "finisher," and previous teachers perhaps never challenged him on staying with a topic for more than one week. He is emblematic of the iPod generation, scrolling through information superficially and digesting only very small amounts before moving on to more information. We were studying brushes and I asked him to find an appropriate tune to play along to in 3/4 (jazz waltz time signature) and prepare for the next lesson. He came in and played a nice version of *Someday My Prince Will Come*. I asked him who the drummer was. He didn't know. But he knew the piano player, Bill Evans. I asked him how and why he selected this particular tune. He said it was next on his iPod library. I smiled. His next assignment was easy… I made him research every drummer that ever played with Bill Evans, in chronological order, and give a brief oral presentation on each one. This took several weeks to accomplish and he began to absorb a slower rhythm of learning and – I hope – started to see the value of staying with one topic for an extended period of time.

You should never be alarmed if a student experiences "practice burnout" or "study overload." The first time it happens, it provides an especially opportune moment to let the student experience a "natural vacation" from his instrument (or the library) and not feel threatened by the need for time away from music or study. I often ask the student what the purpose of any vacation is (family, travel, leisure, reunions), and how many times they have enjoyed such vacations. The same applies to practicing and studying. It is the break from the norm of your routines which enriches and allows you to come back refreshed with renewed vigor and commitment to start working again. The difference in music is that the vacation may not be planned. If the lack of motivation is recurrent, then you must scrutinize both the lack of ambition to work and the issues surrounding it.

In their book *The Elements of Teaching* Banner and Cannon state, "Good teachers always turn experiences that may discourage students into encouraging ones." I have had great success helping students who experience practice burnout or lack of motivation. After having several lengthy discussions with the student to explore all angles of the burnout – its origins, its possible consequences, the inevitable cessation of it, the likely aftermath, and the virtual guarantee of a reoccurrence – there are two possible outcomes. Most times once the burnout period has subsided, the student is again diligently practicing, and a new sense of life is blown into his sail. This renewed vitality and the urge to conquer the burnout all comes from within. There can be no mistake; this is the key. The student returns to practicing because they *want* to do it!

The second scenario, although extreme and less common, is equally important to diagnose and respect. A student enduring burnout may discover that he no longer wishes to pursue a career in music, at the present time, or possibly they may reframe their area of specialization. This in itself is not painful for me, but wonderful, because the student has come much closer to realizing what he really wants to do, and will ultimately be much happier and successful at doing it for having ruled out music and refined his true focus.

You should support either decision with equal poise and encouragement because it is your intent to help identify what is best for that student, whatever it may be. Consequently you should distance yourself from having a vested interest in the student's choosing music. Solely the student must make the decision, and you should not intentionally influence it. Placing the responsibility for the decision in the student's hands will likewise strengthen his ability to make future life decisions. Outcome can never be guaranteed, but effort can be; students must always try their hardest, and yet accept that there are certain factors they cannot control.

A second word that I find much more poignant and am deeply fond of is *inspiration.* Inspiration has greater staying power, and is a direct reflection on your work. It is by EXAMPLE that you should offer yourself to your students in all of your accomplishments and failures so that they can freely draw upon your trials, triumphs, and ongoing self-discovery to motivate and to inspire themselves in their darker or brighter moments. Theodore Roszak states in his book, *The Cult of Information: The Folklore of Computers and the True Art of Thinking*, "Free human dialogue, wandering, wherever the agility of the mind allows, lies at the heart of education. If teachers do not have the time, the incentive, or the wit to prove that; if the students are too demoralized, bored or distracted to muster the attention their teachers need of them, then that is the educational problem which has to be solved – and solved from inside the experience of the teachers and the students."

Inspiration does not happen in a vacuum. Think of all the people who have inspired you. What is it about their achievements and their spirit that attracted you to them? Most of the time, it is simply the path they have chosen, and you wanting to follow suit. It is not so much wanting to be *like them*; rather it is that their achievements can serve as signposts as to what is possible.

You must advocate strongly that students must decide for themselves to work or not to work. This inspiration comes from within and is a renewable source. It draws its strength not from others, but from the deep spiritual reservoir within. Although encouragement from family, friends, and fellow musicians can help an aspiring musician in his darkest moments, it will not sustain him forever. Banner and Cannon state, "Most teachers teach because it gives them the deepest sort of satisfaction. And this is how it should be. It is difficult to imagine effective teachers who do not have abiding fascination with their subjects, who do not love being among students, and who do not gain fulfillment from nourishing other people and their minds."

In the first private lesson of each new semester, I interview my students individually, regardless of whether they are new to my classroom or we have studied together before. I always ask them what they want to work on. Recently I had a new student tell me he wanted me to "make him" transcribe solos. I chuckled and said, "I'm not going *make* you do anything… if you want someone to force you to transcribe solos, find a new teacher…!" He is now in his third semester studying with me and this past spring semester when I interviewed him he said, "I want to start transcribing solos – would you help me?"… I said, "Sure!" with a BIG smile.

As teachers, you must invite your students to follow the paths you have paved, and excite in them a desire to explore beyond the endpoints of your own journeys. They must sincerely want to see the unlimited potential and possibilities in order to pursue them. If you can accomplish this, then you have succeeded, by example, in teaching them to find their own inspiration, deep down inside. You will enable them to draw upon a renewable source within themselves, a well that they alone will be able to revisit and call upon at any time. As Emerson said, "It is not so important what is behind us, or what is ahead of us, but what is inside us."

Chapter Four

VALIDATION

*"Do not become too concerned about what others may think of you.
Be very concerned about what you think of yourself."*

~ John Wooden

No matter what your subject is, your students need to feel comfortable learning from you. Above all, that means they need you to prove that you can teach. But in music, students also seek validation that you can *play*. This proof must be ongoing, and kept anew. For the new student, firsthand observation of your musical performance prompts her to judge you, indirectly, on your merits as a teacher; from this, the student forms a picture of how successful she could become under your guidance.

A returning student who truly understands the nature of performance may overlook a mediocre performance from her teacher, because the performance arena does not directly reflect methodology of teaching. However, the new student who knows nothing of your teaching or has never witnessed you perform will be profoundly affected by what she witnesses that first time. A great performance will be well received and create an open, enthusiastic environment for learning. A poor performance will have disastrous consequences that virtually freeze the student in an unreceptive mode. If you cannot play, how and what can you teach?

I firmly believe that there is too much emphasis put on a teacher in relation to performance. Think of an outstanding coach in sports, now too old to play... agile or not, he remains a great coach with a winning record – that is his validation. What, then, about the teacher who is a great teacher but rarely performs? I guarantee that students will not flock to study with him. In reality, though, such a teacher can be an invaluable resource and an exceedingly good instructor, performer or not. This is especially true in the classical world where "*Master Pedagogue*" is a legitimate title and someone to be sought out. Like the aging coach, a teacher's winning record is his students and their subsequent successful performances and auditions.

Unfortunately, students unfairly will equate a peer's ability to perform to your ability to teach. I do know that students, like everyone else, want results almost immediately. The desire is understandable, and is perhaps (alas) a modern human trait, but results take time. A teacher needs time with a student to accurately assess their abilities. A student's former teachers, personal performance experience, and innate talent quotient reflect the student's composite. Sometimes one lone semester of study with a new teacher whose methodology is unique to a student can impact that student's performance abilities. But most often it requires at least two semesters of diligent practice and an ongoing assimilation of lessons and experiences to really impact how a student performs. To complicate matters, a student's performance can vary depending on how her peers observe it. A student may give a strong performance for the level of experience she has reached, and yet her peers in the audience may judge her harshly, neglecting to consider the gap between their abilities, at present, and hers. Sometimes what they see is not what they are looking at.

Some students are too quick to judge. Not only do they want immediate results in their own playing but they want to witness growth and improvement in others. That way, they can derive inspiration from their peers' successes, and put their own progress into sharper perspective. Unfortunately, not all students are able to appreciate the factors that might make a seemingly mediocre performance they've observed a real triumph for the

VALIDATION

student performing. As the student's teacher you will recognize the progress and the growth, but perhaps no one else will. It is up to you as an educator to impress upon everyone that while comparing one's self to others serves a purpose, success and improvement are relative categories – in music, in writing, in physical education, you name it – and all degrees of achievement warrant respect.

One of the greatest challenges in teaching is recognizing and respecting the initial level of any student that you start with, and realistically gauging and pursuing the final level that you end up with. No one knows these endpoints better than you and that student. A great student may have been great even before studying with a particular teacher – the final result you end up listening to may have nothing to do with that particular teacher!

In my experience I have witnessed many instances of physical and emotional injury to incoming students in the adjustment phase of their first semester. Many times a student is the very best in their hometown. Arriving on campus, they are quick to learn that they are no more than average. It is extremely intimidating to walk down the practice halls and hear 25 incredibly talented musicians, each playing with a degree of passion and precision you previously thought only you possessed. But after the initial shock wears off, the competitive overdrive kicks in, and the student begins to practice countless hours each day to keep up.

You should counsel students not to compare themselves to others. In those first days of class, they know nothing of other students' backgrounds, with whom they might have studied, or how long they have been playing. To impress this upon them I often recite the Zen parable of the young student who wants to become a great swordsman: he asks the master how long it will take to perfect his skills, and the master replies, "Ten years." The student then responds, "If I practice diligently, many hours a day, how long will it take?" and the master replies... "Twenty years." The student then responds, "If I do not eat or sleep, and do nothing but practice, how long will it take?" and the master replies, "Thirty years." The student then says, "But master, why is it that the more I practice, the longer it

RHYTHMIC REFLECTIONS ON CREATIVE TEACHING

takes?" and the master replies, "A student in a hurry learns nothing."

Chapter Five

GRADES

"Pleasure is always all the keener in proportion to the demands of its opposite... painful effort."

~ *The Elements of Teaching*

The greatest burden of responsibility to your students is grading. I have struggled every semester for 25 years attempting to find a formula, or system that works, and I believe there are none. The closer I get to a system that works 90 percent of the time, I have contact with a student that presents a new dilemma or circumstance that makes me rethink my position on grading.

There is no single, greater challenge than the assessment and grading of a student pursuing a degree in Performance Arts. There is not one approach in arriving at a fair grade that can be applied consistently, evenly, and without the threat of bias. I believe a combination of several methods will best support the end result. Objective measures such as final exams and quizzes (despite the appeal their standardized results might offer the conflicted teacher) provide the least support in final grade determination.

However, I do have several guidelines that offer some solace when you must arrive at a fair and objective grade. It is paramount to never forget that while you determine grades in part by comparing students to each other, it is equally important to compare students to *themselves*.

My approach to grading combines three different elements to help fairly assess the student. The first and most crucial is the overall level of the student from day one. His background and potential for growth are key elements in final grade determination. Bill Parcells, the famous football coach, defines potential as "not having done a damn thing." Regardless of Coach Parcells' viewpoint, potential is a necessary element in final grade determination. This is the fairest approach to grading a student, because it measures the student against *himself* and not directly against other students. A simple in-class performance demonstration and ratings audition by an independent panel of colleagues at the beginning of each semester provides a barometer for potential growth.

Secondly, I grade the student on actual work done throughout the semester. Assignments, class participation, attendance, attitude, and exam grades all influence the final grade. Least important in the process is how the student compares to others.

1) **Interview-Assessment**:

   With every new student I meet, whether in class or private lesson, I devote 10 minutes to a discussion of their background. This involves asking how long they have been playing, whether they are self taught or if they had a teacher, what their musical influences might be, and who their favorite musicians are. I then have them play. This allows me to hear where they are at this point in time in relation to their background. It gives me an invaluable starting point by which to gauge their progress in comparison to *themselves* and not others. It also provides some insight into their life story.

2) **Class Work:**

   This is probably the easiest component to grading and the most tangible. A very simple, concrete formula that is applicable in almost all situations weighs "class work" with 20 percent devoted equally as follows: class participation, attendance, attitude, midterm, and final. If I am agonizing over a particular student (generally one teetering between a "D" and "F," passing or failing), starting with this (largely numeric) process usually crystallizes what the student deserves. This is not always what he gets. If the student has demonstrated consistently hard effort and desire to improve, the student will always receive the higher grade no matter what number an average of their test scores might yield. Conversely, a gifted student who works very little and coasts on their own natural talent will potentially receive a low "C" or "D."

3) **Peer Comparison:**
You should never directly compare students to each other, and should put the least weight on how a student performs in relation to others in your classroom. That is because of the great variety of backgrounds and circumstances that a student may come from. I mention to the class what I call "the fruit metaphor" – that all fruit does not blossom at the same time, and there are different growing seasons for each fruit. What is more important is the time spent on cultivating the growth. In this regard effort is more important than results. As psychiatrist Karl Menninger said, "Attitude is more important than facts." Or, as John Wooden reminds us, "We are all the same in having the opportunity to make the most of what we have whatever our situation."

In *The Elements of Teaching*, Banner and Cannon describe the framework of the "tough but fair" approach: "A compassionate regard for students requires setting appropriately high standards in the students' own interest; it is only by challenging students that a teacher reveals true compassion." In this context, passing or failing a student is the ultimate decision, and failing a borderline student is actually more beneficial than passing him. There is no lesson to be learned from barely passing. Failing a student and encouraging him to accept responsibility for his shortcomings offers him the challenge to try to do better the next time. Forcing a student to fight through adversity – rather than sidestepping it with a D-minus – will hopefully instill life-long coping skills and nurture adaptability to life's unforeseen obstacles.

When a student passes with a low grade, it has been my repeated experience that his effort and desire to improve in those weak areas will cease to exist. Neglected areas will continue to be neglected. However, more often than not, when a student fails but is given a second chance, they are determined to succeed. Failing *allows* improvement to unfold; passing does not. It is with continued effort, through repeated failures, that you learn the most. You cannot really be trying your hardest without occasional failures and mistakes. Accomplishment does not necessarily promote continued desire and effort – as the ancient martial arts axiom reminds us, "seven times down, eight times up" is true progress. The one exception I have agreed to, in unique circumstances, is to pass a failing student with a D, with the strict understanding that they will take the class over again. I have never been disappointed when having received this promise from a student. It appears that the absence of grading pressure coupled with more time to digest the material allows the student to blossom in a more comfortable personal rhythm.

Several years ago I was teaching a tiered lab program. There were four levels corresponding to specific weaknesses – technique, fundamentals, style interpretation, and reading. I had a student who I thought was misplaced and would be challenged more if he were moved from level II to III. Since I taught both levels, it was an easy switch to propose. I mentioned this to the student and he was eager to advance. I was very clear that it would be challenging and he would have to spend additional time practicing – I sternly inquired if he could commit to that, and he said yes emphatically.

After several weeks passed and midterms were approaching, it was apparent he was not keeping up with the work. I suggested that he move back to level II, but he insisted he wanted to stay in this class. I said it was his decision, but my best advice was for him to move back to level II because he was in danger of failing. He did fail the midterm, and I told him it was too late to bump back to level II. It was still possible to pass the course but it would take a Herculean effort on his part. He assured me he was up for the task. My intuition told me he was not. The final exam came and he did not pass, and within 10 minutes of completion I received a phone call from his father who went on a tirade blaming me for his son's failure because I was the one who suggested he move up to the next level. After he settled down, I inquired if his son mentioned that I made a mistake in moving him forward to another level and strongly encouraged him to move back. This information was not relayed to his father. I told him I would not pass his son, but I would consider testing him again the following semester. He thought that would be fair.

The following semester came and it was finals time. I briefed a senior colleague on the situation who helped develop the material for the lab programs. I asked him if he would administer the exam and I would be a passive observer. The student failed again, a second time, and I never heard from his father again.

I have failed very few students in my 25 years of teaching. It is not pleasant for either party. You may feel guilty when the only proper course of action is to fail a student, for you must share some of the responsibility for that student's failure. Could you have done a better job? What could you have done differently that may have helped this student pass? These are serious questions teachers must ask themselves. In some cases, this sort of self-critique may lead a teacher to change their approach to presenting certain material in a class, or might even prompt them to eliminate difficult, stale, or extraneous material altogether. As a teacher you must not burden yourself unduly in the shared responsibility, for not all "F" students reflect shortcomings of your knowledge or methodology. The more confidence you develop in time-tested teaching methods, the easier it will be to differentiate between a student you might have let down and one who simply did not commit to practice or studying.

One of the ultimate challenges every teacher will confront is teaching the student you do not blend with or, more bluntly, do not like. It can become even more difficult to grade that student fairly. The just teacher will strive to remain impartial and exhibit the greatest regard for ethical principles of education. How you grade your least favorite student is the moral compass that should direct all other grades. It may be rare that you will encounter a student you do not like, and surely you may have more students through the years who do not like you.

I suggest whenever you struggle to arrive at a particular grade for a borderline student, whom you like a great deal, ask yourself, "What if I didn't like this student?" That is the best quantifier because then you will always err slightly lower in the grade to correct any prejudices on your part. Conversely, with a student you are not particularly fond of, ask yourself "What if I liked this student?" and you might consider giving him a slightly higher grade to compensate for any bias that might creep into your evaluation.

I consider myself to be objective and judicious, almost to a fault. But with the difficulties and emotions that interfere with your objectivity you must continue to explore all possibilities and devices that may ultimately help you to define the progress of your students. It is not an easy task and frankly it does not become easier the more you do it. Reward effort over outcome, be tough, but fair, and you will always determine a grade that both you and your student can live with.

Presently, there is a disease spreading throughout college campuses: grade inflation and, more recently, grade rationing. These alarming trends are interfering with our ability as teachers to grade students properly. Both trends are morally and ethically wrong. The "Bell Curve" has unfortunately been an accepted phenomenon for years now, even though it does little more than use math to justify grade inflation. Worse still, however, is the solution proposed by the (usually) bright minds at Princeton, to control the inflation by binding faculties' hands through grade rationing. Grade rationing, at Princeton, is the distribution of a limited amount of "A" grades a professor is allowed for one specific course, combined with a total allotment for their specific department. I don't know which is more reprehensible – the thought process behind this system, or the eventual outcome that grade rationing will yield.

Another abhorrence is the practice at Loyola Law School, in Los Angeles, of "awarding all students an extra third of a point on their GPAs" to improve their chances of landing a job after graduation. In a recent report by *The New York Times*, at least 10 other schools have "artificially made their grading more lenient." At least "Pass/Fail" grading is honest about what it is. Grade inflation, through rationing or curves or modified GPAs, is nothing more than sanctioned counterfeiting. It is unwarranted and threatens the integrity of all modern academic evaluations.

In this dilemma, we (professors) are both the problem and the solution. It should go no further than that. But it has, with a new trend emerging in which students use the court system to challenge grades. Administrators are equally culpable, and have in several cases changed a student's grade for a class – in some instances without even informing the professor of their involvement. No matter what your role is in the educational system, honesty begins and ends with you. If you cannot be held accountable for your actions and work only to find ways to relieve yourself of the burden of fairly assessing those you teach, how can you expect your students to follow the path of life with an accurate moral compass? They will truly lose their way if they haven't been corrupted already.

Chapter Six

KNOWLEDGE

"The only thing that we can know is that we know nothing and that is the highest flight of human wisdom."

~ Leo Tolstoy

In *The Elements of Teaching*, Banner and Cannon remark that "True teachers always seek to expand their ability to teach. Often they must struggle to learn more, to remain current with what is known about their subjects, to keep those subjects fresh and exciting enough to sustain the exhausting act of teaching day in and day out year after year." There are dangers inherent in the tenure track – tenure can breed complacency, and some teachers lose their initial drive to be constantly evolving and seeking new information to update their craft. To teach well is an endless process... a running brook stays alive by moving. The same is true with teaching.

It's been easy for me to "keep moving" because the desire to improve is an innate part of my being, and I recognize that it strengthens my teaching. It has at times been frustrating when the change I hoped to see did not come quickly, or when my methods for personal improvement did not work. So it may be important and helpful to remind yourself of the concept of vocation as a practice, a perpetual "work in progress" that is evolving, and (hopefully) getting better. It is the ritual of daily practice that is the cornerstone of your pursuit of the elusive goal of perfection. While you may never attain that level, the process is invaluable and will constantly inform you as a teacher striving to keep pace at the forefront of your field.

In my teaching 25 years at Berklee I have taken several courses offered within my department which I felt would focus on my weaknesses. When I first sat down amongst a Berklee class, all of the heads turned in amazement... a *teacher* is taking this class. Their opinion of me was simultaneously diminished and elevated... how could I not know EVERYTHING? And if I did not know everything, should there be a stigma attached to my attempt to fill that void? One should never be intimidated in the quest for greater knowledge. Any attempt to grow, to learn, and to improve as a musician or human being for that matter, should be greeted with support and admiration.

That was the simple lesson I learned sitting down in that classroom as my students' peer, and it was every bit as important as the material I studied in that class. Your willingness to expose your limitations and continued desire for self-improvement applies to student and teacher alike.

It is not uncommon for musicians to attend clinics and master classes. It is, however, uncommon for musicians past a certain point in their careers to continue to study privately with a teacher on their principal instrument. Three years ago I made the decision to study with a local teacher for the summer. He had a very good reputation, and I knew enough of his methodology from students who had studied with him, that I believed I too would benefit from his tutelage – what's more, I was suffering from mild "teacher burnout" and wanted to be the student, for a change.

I am now approaching my third summer of this "continued education," and have benefited every minute from my instructor's concentrated lessons. The additional reward is that the students who hear me practicing new material – like those whose heads turned when I sat myself in a college class – are amazed that I would be still taking lessons, and find new inspiration to concentrate on their own improvement. Your continued commitment to your craft sets an example for them that the process of learning is ongoing.

Recently a student asked me to be part of an informal survey, "What makes a good music teacher?" This is something

I've thought long and hard about, so my response was immediate: "A good music teacher is one who actively performs and practices daily." The student mentioned to me that she found it interesting that I did not say a good teacher is someone who cares about students, someone who is patient, or someone who has multiple solutions to the same problem. My omission was intentional and, I thought, beyond the obvious. These are qualities *inherent* in good teachers – in all areas at all levels of education – they need not be stated. In greater amounts compassion, patience, and careful demonstrations to students are what make up the *best teachers*!

What makes a good football player? It's automatically understood he loves the game. What makes a great chef? She loves to cook and eat. Unfortunately, some of my colleagues have a disdain for teaching and still continue to teach. A chef who dislikes her profession could not possibly prepare as fine a meal, nor a quarterback who no longer loves his sport throw as accurate a spiral. Above all, to teach effectively you must love to teach. Banner and Cannon state, "If the fire of knowledge is extinguished in teachers, even the best students are unlikely to reignite the torch and carry it to its ultimate destination."

Popularity should not define good teaching nor should it influence the content of what you teach. Diluting the curriculum you teach may increase your popularity among students, but it will compromise your integrity and jeopardize educational focus. A colleague of mine once complained that his "popularity" was decreasing because he was too strict with his students. He wanted to soften his approach, which in a small dose may not have been a bad idea. But I suggested to him that he had been popular with his students up until this point precisely because of his strict approach, and that perhaps his popularity had diminished for a different reason. I suggested that perhaps he was unhappy with teaching, and simply needed a break (a sabbatical) to refocus. One year later, after a rejuvenating sabbatical, my colleague returned, made a minor adjustment to his teaching style, and found himself more popular than ever.

RHYTHMIC REFLECTIONS ON CREATIVE TEACHING

A teacher who is unpopular for a myriad of reasons may attempt to increase his popularity by diluting his syllabus to attract more students, but many more students will end up less informed. Tough love is always essential; so is staying true to what you know. John Wooden emphatically states, "Knowledge alone is not enough to get desired results."

As a teacher, you should never be intimidated by what you do not know. Conversely, a colleague who may be considered an "expert" in a specific style and whose knowledge might be greater than yours should not feel threatening to you. It is important not just to share what you know, but also to share it in the *way that you know it*. There is great strength in that. No one knows exactly the same things, in exactly the same way that you know them. Teachers draw upon who they are, and what they know. Who you are and what you know are inseparable from what and how you teach. Ideally you should teach as you live... or as Oscar Wilde humorously reminds us, "Be yourself, everyone else is taken."

It is vital to honor what students want, yet equally important to balance it with what they need! Each new semester (in private lessons), I embark upon a mutually agreed program of study for the coming year, then I let the student decide each week what they want to focus on in their lesson. If the student over several weeks avoids a particular topic, then I need to question his avoidance of that topic. This fosters responsibility. The student at this critical juncture needs to be held accountable both for what he *is* practicing and for what he *is not* practicing. With the passage of time, specific goals and targeted topics of study may no longer be important to that student, and that is okay to a point, so long as he is upfront with you about why he chooses to avoid the topic in question.

Continuity and consistency are primary ingredients in improving weak areas and perpetuating self-growth. Events during the course of a semester may lead to a reevaluation of specific goals. In some (rare) instances students may wish to alter their intended course of study completely which may run contrary to your teaching philosophies, and may even require knowledge that extends beyond your expertise. It requires a tremendous amount of sensitivity and experience to know when to deviate from your own set curriculum in order to honor a student's request to explore a specific topic. It takes even greater care and caution to approve a student's deviation from a set path of study that was previously agreed upon. Depending on the reasons he gives, you may be wise to offer resistance to the student's desire to "change course."

Bruce Lee said, "A teacher is never a giver of truth; he is a guide, a pointer to the truth that each student must find for himself." Whatever the issues are though, simply asking about and absorbing the student's reasons will never fail to provide you with valuable information to help you guide that student in the best direction to suit her present needs. After hearing the student out, it is important to state your own opinion even if it runs counter to the student's desire to change her educational direction.

Ultimately, letting the student decide will increase their share of educational responsibility, and will likewise increase your flexibility to the ever-changing needs of your students. If the new topic is beyond your scope or expertise, then you must point that student toward another teacher – this takes courage, but is absolutely necessary.

Similarly, you should encourage students to disagree, and to speak up if they have been told something different than what you try to impart to them. "Let's talk about it" is a simple invitation that encourages open dialogue. The best way for students to learn is to be presented with a variety of opinions, and then allowed to determine for themselves the appropriate answer.

It is important to stress that perspective evolves with the passage of time, and so both the question and answer may change. Perhaps the greatest source of information that students possess is within them! The key as a teacher is learning when and how to tap into that knowledge, and how to integrate information students already possess as an additional resource. I make it a point to have an early office hour, at 8:00 AM. This honors many of my core philosophies. I am a morning person. My mind and ears are fresher on the heels of a sunrise. The students who really want something of me outside of class will discover that it requires very little effort to find the source. Those students who have a difficult time getting up early may find the journey more challenging, but will find the reward far greater. An early office hour generally filters out those who want to learn from those who don't. As added inducement I always offer to buy coffee. I make concessions and propose alternative times by appointment for those students that work nights, commute from a distance, or have family obligations. But there is no excuse for not wanting to learn.

It reminds me of the Zen parable where the Zen student wanted to study with a particular master, and had to wait outside the gate because the master was not there. The student was told to go home, but would not leave, and waited until the next day. He was then told the same thing. He still would not leave. Spring turned to summer, summer to fall, fall turned to winter... each day he was told the same thing: "The master is not here; come back tomorrow." Two years later when spring arrived the master finally agreed to meet with him and simply remarked that he wanted to see how strong the student's desire to learn was. My early office hour serves the same function in a more subtle and manageable way. It allows students to demonstrate to me their desire to learn.

Tomo was the rare exception. Tomo was an overly devoted student where his eagerness to learn and impress me was not to his benefit. The student was from Japan where having a *sensei* carries a great weight of responsibility and honor for student and teacher alike. Tomo was my private student for one hour, in my jazz ensemble for two hours, and in two other classes one hour each. This in itself was excessive. The problem was Tomo started coming to my office hour exactly at 8:00, waiting at my door. I always made him wait five or 10 minutes so I could quickly do my warm-ups and organize what I needed to do that day. When he came in, there was not a lot of new knowledge that was waiting to be unearthed, and he was not struggling with any specific course-related difficulties. Tomo needed more practice time by

KNOWLEDGE

himself and less time with me. This trend continued well into the semester. I even tried to get to my office before he did to start my warm-ups and perhaps not be able to hear his polite knock. He figured that out and started getting to my office before me at 7:30!

One time he came to a jazz trio gig I had and sat in. The bass player remarked, "He sounds like a baby Hazilla." That was not a compliment to me, despite its intention. Tomo needed to find his own voice. At my next office hour, I asked Tomo why he came every week. He said because he wanted to learn and I was his teacher. I tried to be gentle in my dissuasion and told him that I was honored by his devotion to me but sometimes after the seed is planted, it is best for it to grow away from the shadow of the farmer. After our talk, his early morning visits became less frequent.

One must be willing to take joy and comfort in the growth and success of former students. You must not become bitter or jealous if a pupil of yours goes on to achieve in ways you failed to do; rather, you should rejoice and relish the success of those you helped teach. Let their achievements serve as inspiration and motivation for your present students, and know that each success validates your methodologies and approach to teaching. Students, in return, should never forget former teachers, no matter how far they progress.

It reminds me of the time that I was humbly embarrassed for failing to acknowledge my first drum teacher Tony Monforte, and I deserved the shame. Every spring Tony produced a show called Drumarama. It was an elaborate six-hour production that featured all of his present students and a few select former students. I was asked to perform and to submit an updated bio. Foolish me, I did not include *his* name in my list of mentors, but included the names of many more famous drummers. At the end of the show, with a brown paper bag over his head with eyeholes cut out, and the words "NO NAME DRUM TEACHER" scrawled on the outside, he called me aside (ever the teacher) to give me my honorarium. Words were not necessary. If it weren't for Tony I would not be where I am today, and it was one of my greatest lessons in life to be humbly reminded of how selflessly he taught me. I thank him for that. As *Zen Guitar* teaches us, "We are all students and teachers in everything we do and we are both at the same time. When a child learns from the parent, the parent learns from the child. Each imparts different lessons." There would be no teachers without students, and no students without teachers.

Chapter Seven

ROLE MODEL

"I never had one specific 'moment' with Alan that changed my life and music, rather my life and music were forever changed the moment I met him."

~ Jon Hazilla on Alan Dawson

This chapter should provoke a stimulating debate and I would like to approach it on three distinct levels:

1) The student's perception of you as teacher/performer, by word of mouth and in the privacy of a lesson or class.

2) The student's perception of you after they witness you perform, and how they relate to what you teach. Are you as good a performer as you are a teacher? Is the material you teach, and how you teach it, directly visible in your playing? Does it reflect who you are?

3) Does your popularity underscore or undermine your ability to be a quality teacher? Do you alter the content of what you teach in order to appeal to a broader base of students, and, if so, do you thereby dilute the import of what you teach?

Most musicians are aware of the difficulties of live performances, the fluctuation of circumstances, and the simple fact that you do not play at your best level all the time. It can be a valuable lesson for students to experience by observing you in the teacher/performer role. A great performance by a teacher does not need an explanation. Does a poor one?

Any student in specialized study "one on one" who is in close contact with you over the period of a semester may develop a small dependency. A student may even come to idolize you, viewing you as "the best and greatest" ... and a teacher may well be that, and more. If you are making the correct diagnosis of the student's problem areas and are suggesting proper corrections, and if the student diligently practices and then witnesses results, a sort of veneration seems almost natural, and only strengthens the bond that exists between you.

Unfortunately, the sort of "hero worship" that can occur in the classroom or in private lessons puts greater pressure on you as the teacher. Much of the reverence students exhibit during their lessons is carried over to witnessing you in a performance role... and the same high expectations are again placed upon you, now as the performer.

Numerous questions arise here, as well as the potential for several problems. If you have a poor performance does that undermine the student's perception of you as a sort of invincible musical talent? How does a poor performance then affect your ability to communicate lessons to the student? Will the student have less confidence in you now that he has witnessed a performance in which, it seemed, the fruits of many years of expert practice failed to fully ripen? Does it affect the student's ability to continue to believe in you and your methods of instruction, if they do not appear to help you in actual performance?

What is the student to believe if this fragile relationship with you doesn't equal in performance what has been so worthy of admiration in the classroom and private lessons? And perhaps the most difficult question of all, how do you explain to the student your poor performance and its relevance to good teaching?

Many years ago I was the director for a concert honoring one of my former teachers, Joe Morello, who was known for filling the drum chair in Dave Brubeck's Quartet and for his incredible drum solo on Dave Brubeck's jazz hit "Take Five." Part of my study for this program was learning a difficult snare etude book titled *Portraits In Rhythm* by Anthony Cirone. The irony was I would stumble through the etudes, while Joe – who is legally blind – would correct me from memory… he literally had the book memorized! As homage to him in the concert, I attempted to memorize one of his favorite etudes.

I spent three months in preparation learning and memorizing the complex rhythmic phases. I played it for colleagues and solicited their feedback. Concert night I was ready. And in front of 1,000 people in the Berklee Performance Center I attempted to play the piece… I started… and managed to play the first few lines poorly… then my mind went blank. I had no memory. I stopped, and apologized to Joe and the audience and started from the beginning… this time I made it halfway through… and my mind went blank again. I was humiliated and embarrassed. I stopped again and started one more time, from the top, determined to play the etude from memory. It was not to be. I played two-thirds of the way through and my mind went blank again. Relying on jazz sensibilities and strong practice in improvisation I managed to recreate the spirit of the recapitulation… but it was not note for note perfect. Only two people knew that and a lone voice above the rousing applause graciously shouted out "Great job!" We both knew it was not.

The Elements of Teaching tells us: "The teachers who we remember the most vividly, are those who knew their subjects best and transmitted them with the greatest intensity and love. They were confident in their knowledge and not dogmatic; they acted out their own struggles to understand in front of us, joyful when they understood something fresh, troubled when they did not or could not know."

As teachers, you must firmly believe that you cannot impart your knowledge with "intensity and love" if you do not both a) engage in a daily practice routine, and b) actively perform. In teaching any of the performance arts or visual arts the same would be true. Is it even possible in today's economic world, to be both a good teacher and a good performer? Yes, if you can maintain an equal balance of dedication and integrity to both. Unfortunately performance and touring tends to take precedence over teaching at the literal expense of your students. In fairness to your students, should you maintain one foot in each realm, or make a decision to be one or the other, but not both?

Banner and Cannon suggest a sort of happy medium. "Teachers should not be self-conscious about revealing how knowledge has enriched their own lives and how teaching is an expression of their desire to enrich others' lives too. On the contrary: they should try to exemplify the deep pleasure which their own continuing learning brings them." To extend their thought, you are the best example of what you teach and how you teach. Teaching by example when you are the example is the most effective way to teach. Your success in the classroom and beyond will depend on how your students perceive you as examples in both arenas.

In the ancient text of the Talmud there is a saying: "We do not see things as they are, we see them as we are." I am known as a demanding teacher with very high standards. This emanates from a place inside of me. I employ the set of standards to which I hold myself as the measuring stick for my students' efforts. I do not expect anything from my students that I have not done myself (or that I am not continuing to do), be it in practice, during performance, or in life. Your successes and failures are the best examples you can offer your students in your continued desire to learn and improve. You must remember that at one time, you too were students and in a sense, you never stop being students.

As teachers, your role invariably transcends the purely academic, and arises to that of personal "counselor." To my students, I always offer my compassionate listening skills – developed through training as a lay minister – to let them vent about girlfriend/boyfriend problems, a bad ensemble, or just general school malaise. Sometimes an entire lesson may be devoted to talking about a personal problem unrelated to music, and this is time well spent. If the problem is serious, you must not only be extremely sensitive, but should urge the student to seek counseling from a trained professional on the school staff. I am always glad to make the initial phone call (this first step is often the hardest for students) so that the student can be in contact with the counseling office. I will also maintain a watchful eye, week by week, just to monitor the student's progress and, when necessary, I will make sure that a student did in fact follow through with an appointment.

If the student is suffering from general burnout, you should immediately inquire about the student's involvement with hobbies and exercise. Such constructive diversions are a vital part of any successful career in music and in life, and are indispensable ingredients for a nourishing existence.

I have been running for 25 years, and have found that it has enhanced every aspect of my life. You should strongly encourage your students to engage in some form of exercise... biking, walking, swimming: whatever works for them. I often share with my students the list of my top three priorities in life: health, family, and music. It never fails to amaze them that music is third and health is number one – but if you are sick, nothing matters other than getting better. When fighting off an illness, it is the right time to become selfish – for the sake of your health, your relationships, and your music. If you are sick, you don't spend the day practicing or thinking about your next performance, nor do you immerse yourself in the company or family or friends. You cannot fully enjoy or thrive in any aspect of your life when you are sick. Even for someone who lives and breathes music, health must be the top priority.

I have offered to students many articles from my health files on nutrition, vitamins, meditation, and running when our conversations reveal their lives would be dramatically enhanced by these changes. It also solidifies a deeper personal bond and connection that I develop with the student that transcends the musical environment.

Exercise also offers a full retreat from your chosen craft. It allows balance, focus, and clarity to permeate into your daily musical life. I've often been inspired on my long runs to come up with my next creative musical project. I've also weathered many a stressful day by running and "creative problem solving" during the 45 minutes I spend on my exercise routine. Although running may not be for them, you should emphasize to your students some form of exercise should be. In music as in life, regular exercise is an asset beyond measure.

Many times students have difficulty organizing their practice routines. If a student has an established history of loosely organized study, halfhearted lessons, and poor practice habits, then the pattern will not change much without a highly concentrated effort both from the student and the teacher.

My first suggestion to overcome this loose structure is for students to keep a practice journal. This simple log allows them to see what they practice, what they don't practice, and what they *think* they practice. After a week or so, you should have them begin to keep track of what they consider to be a realistic amount of time they can practice each day, taking into account the natural fluctuations of school course load, performances, study for unrelated topics, and personal time. Finally, have students identify their strengths and weaknesses, and together you can target specific areas that need to be prioritized over other areas that simply need routine maintenance.

Have your students write out a one-week goal, a one-month goal, a one-year goal, a five-year goal, and a ten-year goal. The shorter-term goals are meant to psychologically boost their confidence, to discourage procrastination, and to foster a sense that objectives can be accomplished if realistically set forth and diligently pursued. The short-term goals also introduce a regimented structure to their practice. The long-term goals are meant to inspire them to "stay the course" in the direction of their ultimate aspirations, but at the same time to be open to the possibility of these goals shifting or changing over time.

As discussed previously, one of the problems with the teaching of music is that many teachers rely on teaching as their primary income source, yet do not put their heart into the profession out of hidden resentment that they are not self-sufficient, full-time performers. This all too common phenomenon raises the question, is it too difficult to be both a successful performer and a successful teacher? In sports, advancing age dictates natural retirement from active participation. The one-time player who yearns to stay close to the game can simply redirect his focus, and perhaps become a head coach in the same league. This secondary position provides him with an extended career beyond playing.

Should music also have a set retirement from active performance so that you may best concentrate on teaching? But how can anyone so in love with music not continue to play? And if you do forge ahead with your playing, is it acceptable not to be at the top of your craft, to play with something less than the speed and finesse you exhibited in your prime, say 20 years before?

As teachers you must forever remain students, but you cannot forever remain young, and there is a critical difference. You must embrace the natural life change of aging and recognize the rewards that accompany it. Age comes with the passage of time. It is unavoidable. But how does it (and *should* it?) affect your teaching? Does the aging process make your teaching better, mellower, richer? Does a diminishing performance career undermine your ability to teach, or might this "decline" actually heighten your ability to instruct others in the discipline you once mastered?

Banner and Cannon in *The Elements of Teaching* sum up the point: "Teachers ought to feel free to allow their changing selves to enter the classroom." If you are graceful as you age and openly accept the process, if you confront it with honesty and welcome the wisdom it crystallizes, then surely you will *enhance* your relationship with your students. They continue: "Compassion is inherent... in teaching because teachers share with their students a sense of frustration, regret, and pain at the difficulties and struggles they must undergo to learn." Aging is simply one more shared struggle, and your composure in the face of it is one more lesson.

Life is an ongoing struggle. Teaching, too, is a struggle – sometimes less than others. But it is in these struggles that you learn things about life that enrich your teaching. You cannot tell your students which path to take, only the ones that you have taken. Or, as Woody Guthrie said, "Take it slow, but take it." I would say, take any path slowly, but take a path.

Chapter Eight

COMMUNICATION

"What we have here is a failure to communicate…"
~ The Warden, *Cool Hand Luke*

The art of communication is paramount in successful teaching. If a teacher is unable to communicate a single idea with a myriad of interpretations, that teacher's message is doomed. What one student easily grasps may be incomprehensible to others. The teacher's ability to reframe the answer or question will be the factor that differentiates between success and failure in educating young minds. (A note of caution when teaching students with ADD: reframing the question and answer may only add to confusion rather than providing clarity.)

As a teacher it is your job to restate (with the utmost patience), as many times as needed, in as many ways as possible, the same information to the students who don't "get it." As Banner and Cannon put it, "Persistence (must be) allied with a determination to help others learn… patience is one of the elements of teaching."

When every other means of getting your point across has failed, enlisting another student to help explain the answer usually works, but should be used as a last resort, and never because you are too frustrated to continue trying to connect with your confused pupil. It is important to gain the trust of students; entrusting an explanation to a sharp student during class – and empowering him to impart it to a peer struggling to understand – can kindle a deep trust between teacher and student. And it's true, too, that the same solution – explained differently or from a different source – sometimes finds more open ears.

Teaching "student to student," you might inquire if students know of a different way to arrive at a solution to a problem. When you have had difficulty explaining an answer, you should turn to the students for their ideas, and you will never be disappointed. It is remarkable that a student can recite to his peer virtually the same information that you tried to impart and have it be received successfully when that same information did not resonate at all when delivered by you. Students' minds sometimes travel in markedly similar wavelengths, and yet try as you might to relate, your plane will always be slightly apart from theirs. Contrary to popular conception, this disconnect is not regrettable; it is, in fact, part of the solution to a common academic problem. Sometimes information is more readily digestible when it comes from within the same peer group than from a source of authority.

Trust is a key element to any exchange of knowledge. Without trust, no matter what we say or how we say it, our words will never be absorbed, understood, or pondered after the fact. Trust evolves gradually over time, and matures through daily teaching. Your punctuality, organization, attendance, and fairness to all students – if witnessed daily – will build trust. Nothing else can replace that process, nor can it be fast-forwarded.

Chemistry in the classroom is a less tangible element of the overall dynamic, but it is also based on trust. Encouraged properly, it can be a very effective tool for learning. In music, this is best accomplished by having the students play an exercise in which the success of the group depends upon each individual student's ability to execute a given passage. This activity is called "chain building" and plays out in a "round" or "cannon" approach. You may have them individually play two or four bar phrases of a snare etude form beginning to end. Collectively the entire class performs the etude as if "one student played it."

This is an invaluable teaching tool that allows you to concentrate on each individual student. It allows you to focus

COMMUNICATION

on the importance of each individual phrase and its importance to the larger whole. This is critically important, as students rarely hear or listen beyond their own phrase. Playing in a round changes all of that. It's a profound lesson in music and in life.

Sometimes when I employ this method of teaching, I will threaten students (in a transparently playful way!) by insisting that class will not be dismissed until they are able to play through the entire exercise without stopping. (Mistakes are allowed but stopping isn't!) It's amazing how the spirit of helping one another blossoms in this setting. Some students begin to play other students' parts (overlap) to help them get through a difficult passage. If a student is struggling through the exercise because she didn't practice enough, this approach motivates her to practice more in anticipation of the next class (because who wants to be the weak link?). It also draws mild attention to them and where they fit in with the class.

Finally, this exercise suggests to each person in the class that a team practice may be in order. Generally, after you first introduce the chain exercise, several students will get together outside of the classroom and practice to ready themselves for the next meeting. This fosters a sort of inter-student "mentoring" in which weaker students pair with stronger ones. Because the students themselves initiate this move toward teamwork, and because it serves explicitly to extend the exchange of knowledge beyond the confines of the classroom (and beyond your scope of intervention and observation), it is truly a wonderful phenomenon. You will always be touched as a teacher to know that you've inspired it.

A suggestion to extend or vary the "team" concept and continue to foster the spirit of personalization is to resist the excessive use of handouts in private instruction – the value of those lessons stems from interaction and guidance, not from extraneous papers. You may on occasion want to use handouts in classroom situations, like pre-planned exercises or an article from a publication. In specific circumstances where the handout relates directly to your lesson plan, having the students digest the information in a handout makes sense, and is appropriate. A uniform principle or technique that is articulately explained in an article is well worth distributing in a classroom, and can be circulated without compromising the integrity of your teaching or infringing on copyright issues.

In all cases, books are mandatory for specific classes. In general though I prefer the "hands-on" method of teaching, and never resort to a photocopy when working with a pupil one on one. It is far preferable to have each student take her own personal notes that we can review together at the end of each lesson. How could a predetermined photocopy be as relevant to a one-on-one lesson as a teacher and student's notes on the session?

In my private teaching I have several concepts that I routinely introduce to students. One example is *full strokes* (this concept is drummer specific). This is a very simple exercise in explanation, but difficult in execution. It would be much easier to collect my thoughts on paper, briefly explain the exercise to my student, and then hand him an accompanying handout. Yet I intentionally avoid this shortcut! Instead, writing directly into the student's own notebook, I hand-draw a rough schematic of the student's hand, and pencil a word-for-word explanation of the exercise alongside the sketch exercise.

The content and diagram change very little from student to student, but that does not excuse the shortcut of a photocopy. The point is, you want each student to understand and to feel that they are unique both in their abilities, and the learning process, no matter how broad the study may seem or how readily available a generic solution may be to you as the teacher. Their reinforced individuality, coupled with my deep caring for their musical and personal growth, forms the initial step in a bond of trust. This approach subtly encourages students to grow and practice at their own unique pace. This bond might not develop with an impersonal photocopy or a programmed explanation.

Banner and Cannon aptly observe that "Teaching is a fiduciary act... the ethical components of teaching require teachers to put themselves in their students' places, to imagine the confusions of their students and their desires to be guided toward their own good. Teachers must recall their own earlier vulnerabilities." Many times when teaching a lower-level student, you might try and remember back 10, 15, or 20 years to recall what it was like to be at that stage yourself. Patience is a vital part of helping a struggling student improve and provides invaluable insight into the student's difficulty at that precise moment. You must immediately identify with the student at the exact level of talent at which she's stuck. That is easier said than done. For any advanced percussion teacher, the automatic response mechanism (or "muscle memory") is so strong in your own playing that it is difficult to "unlearn" your expertise in order to match the student's talent level. This is true in more disciplines than just music. Unlearning the conjugation of an irregular verb in a foreign language, thinking back to a time when you hadn't yet read about a specific part of history, or trying to recall what it felt like to struggle with a physics formula is just as difficult – and just as important.

One suggestion specific to my teaching from a fellow colleague was to practice with the reverse hands or feet while drumming. This might be analogous to teaching first or second graders how to write or print letters; assuming you are right-handed, you might try printing or writing left-handed in order to mimic the challenge this new undertaking poses for the child. As a teacher, you have been writing for years upon years... how can you recapture a moment in time that no longer exists? You can't turn back the hands of time, but you can certainly capture a *feeling* in the present that will enable you to understand once again the difficulties inherent within something that seemed anything but simple 25 or 30 years ago.

Sharing in your students' favorite music also allows you to create a sort of mental reference catalog from which you can make a specific connection to a particular student's favorite drummer during a lesson or class. You will find that students really respond to this connection because they're impressed that you remember their favorite drummer and that you knew that work well enough to draw on or make the comparison; moreover they will invariably relate to your example better simply because you tied it to a musician they know and enjoy.

This is one reason you should make it a point every first class to go around the room and have the students share this information. They should introduce themselves, say where they are from, and share who their favorite drummers and biggest influences are. This usually forms an instant bond between students who are either from the same hometown or share a favorite drummer.

From a selfish standpoint, this introduction consistently exposes you to new music and new drummers, and allows you to familiarize yourself with artists and styles that you might not ordinarily listen to. Make it a point to borrow a student's favorite CD if you have not heard of that particular drummer or group. Without exception, your students will be impressed that you show such a sincere interest in their music. This gesture sets the stage, too, for those students whose music you've studied on your own time to be more receptive to what you have to offer to their playing style and abilities in the weeks ahead.

It is also important that you reveal your own musical background and favorite drummers to the class, so the students can begin to relate to you (and not just each other) on the same important level. I firmly believe that who you are as a person will be who you are as a teacher. The two are inseparable. This idea is reflected further in this verse: "No written word, nor spoken plea, can teach our youth what they should be… Nor all the books, on all the shelves… It's what the teachers are themselves." All of us have flaws, and surely some of our own innate characteristics may not be among the essential qualities for excellence in teaching. You should make every effort to improve upon those weak points in yourself. While perfection can never be realized, it is virtually impossible to be a tyrant or a scatterbrain in real life, and yet emerge from your cocoon into the classroom as a focused, sensitive teacher.

There are many styles of teaching, and no one way to teach. Conversely there are equally as many styles of learning, which makes it essential to identify your approach to teaching and maintain the course. In most cases, students will seek you

COMMUNICATION

out based on reputation. Because of their learning style, they will gravitate toward an appropriately compatible teaching style. Do not change your approach to accommodate a student. If you change your style or blend different teaching methods to accommodate a student, you will ultimately be less effective because you are no longer being true to your inner core of *how* you convey knowledge. Your approach will be diluted and everyone will suffer from that compromise. More importantly, you will start to attract the wrong types of students (at least, for you) based on their misconception of who you are as a teacher.

In Robert Pater's book *The Black Belt Manager*, he refers to the martial arts as entailing a "time to penetrate and a time to yield... be rock not water and be water not rock." So too with teaching. One must be flexible one moment, and firm the next. It is the intuitiveness of knowing when and how much of each to display that will differentiate between mediocrity and excellence in the classroom. If you can be consistent in how you maneuver between flexibility and firmness then you can ensure that you continue to attract high-caliber students whose learning styles are ideally suited in your methods.

There are four types of students identified in the ancient Jewish text *Mishnah*: the sponge, the funnel, the strainer, and the sieve. The sponge absorbs, the funnel receives at one end and spills out the other, the strainer lets the wine drain through and retains the dregs, and the sieve is the best for it lets out the flour dust and retains the fine flour.

Perhaps one of the most difficult challenges of teaching is instructing the less-talented student. This task, no matter how arduous, is worthy of your most concerted and passionate efforts. Despite the inherent difficulty, it is the greatest reward in teaching to achieve success where other teachers have failed. It strengthens your resolve and reinforces your teaching approach because you have succeeded in the most impressive way – by reaching what was thought to be unreachable.

I was recently co-teaching a course. The course had been in existence for some time, and the other teacher, despite his skill, seemed to have made little effort to update the course over the years. It was natural for me to question the material I was presenting. The syllabus and outline, written long ago by the other teacher, felt dated, and there was no modern textbook to supply the class with fresh ideas. I felt divided about whether to supply my own materials to supplement his stale approach, or whether to try to adhere to his original course outline and objectives.

Striking a happy medium seemed ideal, but this was easier said than done. Taking a step back to look at my predicament, I found that my problems were multiplying. I invariably wound up comparing myself to this lead teacher, who was a very popular man and an excellent musician... that was a big mistake! I began to think too much about whether the students would accept the material or would like the way the class was structured. I felt I needed to consult the students directly about the material and their interest in it, and I wound up doing this almost obsessively. This is not uncommon when you begin to teach a class that already has a set curriculum that you did not design. The real problem however was this: I subconsciously placed too much value on the students' thoughts and became too worried about being accepted by them and providing them with materials they would like. As a teacher, you sometimes need to exercise judgment and dictate the material that would best serve students' educational growth. If previous standard material has served you well, it will serve them well, if given the chance.

This is a perfect example of a time where you must make the decisions based on what you believe to be best for your students. You cannot bend your ideals and blindly pander to the students' desire for a revised curriculum. Remember, what students want and what they need is often different! Unpopular current decisions may have long-term benefits if given a chance. But how could I convince the students of this, and encourage them to work with me, even though many of them were unmotivated by the syllabus?

I started with a simple seating modification. The room was visually too bright and austere, and most importantly there was no center of attention. In this class, we were sitting in a semi-circle, an arrangement I'd found to work well in the past (and a set-up I still prefer). A big part of my teaching philosophy is to emphasize that all told, I am just like my students. The semi-circle breaks down the student/teacher wall leaving less authority and less intimidation. One of my problems with this particular class, however, was that I was perceived as "one of them." I needed to demonstrate, if only visually, that while I was their peer on one level, I was nevertheless their teacher.

I needed to change my physical space in relation to them. I began sitting at a desk and conducting at least a portion of the class from there. It made a huge difference. The tone and attention of the class changed entirely. The students were less argumentative than they had been, and when they did challenge me on an issue (which I encourage), I found there was more substance in their contentions.

I gradually became more demanding of my students, and clearer about what I expected of the class. I started to play the drums myself more often in class. Since this was a required high-level performance-based course, I emphasized student performance more, and tried to lead by example. I always played demonstrations in other classes, so why not this one? I admit, I was intimidated at first, and had to reestablish myself musically in relation to them. I felt I had to prove myself to them as a performer. I had worked to earn their respect in the classroom; now, I felt I must validate it through performance. Through my seating modifications, a clearer vision of expected coursework, and an increase in personal performance demonstrations, this class responded almost immediately and in the end I gained their respect.

Neil Postman in his book *The End of Education* said that you can "become a different person because of something you have learned; you can appropriate an insight, a concept, a vision so that your world is altered." In order to deliver a message that can make this profound a difference, an insight so deep as to alter someone's worldview, you must first command respect. No one is deserving of respect without proven previous merit. You warrant respect as a musician if your career boasts significant accomplishments, you've "grown old with your instrument," and yet you've retained the humbleness you had long ago as a student. As a teacher, your students' respect for you is based on your previous accomplishments, coupled with your daily presentations on stage or in the classroom. Students may know very little about you as a teacher or mentor prior to meeting you (though it is more likely they will have a feel for your style through word of mouth), but whether they have preconceived notions about your abilities or not, you have the opportunity to build a bridge of respect starting on the first day of class.

Conversely you may never build that bridge without a slow, methodical presentation of who you are. If you attempt to force respect on a student, it will instantly be revoked and evaporate. You cannot look for respect; respect will find you. Respect can only be proven or earned. Without it, the things you say and do to teach those around you will never find their mark or succeed in reshaping a student's worldview.

In my formative years of teaching, I questioned many things about my approach. It made sense, since my young colleagues and I cumulatively had "zero teaching experience." With the passage of time and the refinement of my techniques, I have come to be known as a very capable and educationally strict teacher. I impose very high standards on my students. I have no patience for tardiness or forgetfulness; both are bad educational and life practices. To be late is disrespectful, and to forget something because you did not bother to write it down is irresponsible.

You cannot instantly become a good teacher the first day – or year – of teaching. Through trial and error and the aid of time, you become a *better* teacher. I knew early on that I possessed the common ingredients and qualities to be a successful teacher. I had a strong passion to teach, a caring nature, patience, flexibility, an open mind, and the ability to articulate the simplest answers to the most difficult questions. I knew that my early struggles, if surrounded by patience, and the gift to communicate would soon flower into a rich garden. There is an old Zen saying, "When the student is ready the teacher will appear." The garden is ready now, so please help with the harvest.

Chapter Nine

FRIENDSHIP

"We may disagree, but may we agree to disagree, and still be friends."

~ Unknown

In *The Elements of Teaching*, Banner and Cannon use the word "authority" for their discourse in a chapter. They define *authority* as "legitimate influence over others." While this may be true in the armed forces and at lower grade levels, I could not disagree more fervently with its application at the college level. I prefer the word *respect*. More importantly, if you have the students' respect you will undeniably have the invisible power of authority over them by default, and this you will rarely need to invoke. It is possible to have authority merely by virtue of what you represent within the teacher/student dichotomy, but exerting your authority this way, you may never have your students' respect. Authority always follows respect; respect never follows authority.

Banner and Cannon continue: "Teachers may be students' instructors, advisors, confessors, audiences, cheerleaders, even idols; such mentors may, indeed should, show compassion and empathy, reveal the pleasures of sharing and learning with younger people, and extend warmth and friendly affection. But teachers should never be students' close friends or companions, never their intimates." I diverge even further from this point of view. Although it is extremely difficult to keep friendship separate from your teacher/student role, it is possible if you remain continually mindful that your first responsibility is to mentor.

There is nothing wrong with developing a close bond with a student – it not only fosters an increased respect, but enhances the learning environment. Outright friendships with students should be discouraged. However, if a friendship does develop, it is your duty to be prudent in its development, and to closely monitor how far we allow that heightened bond to extend into the classroom. It is your responsibility, not the student's, to draw the line. And you must at all times remain vigilant not to let that friendship in any manner influence or hinder the learning process of that student.

Perhaps the most difficult aspect of a friendship between a student and a teacher is the unintended and almost unconscious influence this bond can exert on procedural issues which require rigid judgment (grading, deadline extensions for unusual circumstances, prerequisite waivers, etc.). How do you navigate this issue? *Consistency* is the key. What you do for one student, you must do for all. Do not make any exceptions for basic procedure modifications like those mentioned above. If you carefully *explain* your logic on these issues to the student, it is usually accepted with little resistance.

Compassion is a strong word, particularly in relation to teaching, and it should be reflected upon. To quote again from *The Elements of Teaching*, "Compassionate regard for students requires setting appropriately high standards in the students' own interest... to become known by students as tough, but fair is one of the crowning achievements of teaching... teachers should not be their students' closest friends, but students need to feel that their teachers are approachable and interested in their lives as well as learning." Recently a new student arrived extremely late for his lesson. I could tell he was preoccupied and distraught. I was reluctant to inquire what was wrong since I did not know him that well. But he volunteered he was in the emergency room with his wife, who had a severe migraine. He was profusely apologetic for his tardiness; I said there was no need to be considering his circumstance. It was a perfect moment to inquire what he valued most in life. Without hesitation, he said music. I was surprised and as time ran out I

FRIENDSHIP

asked him to "re-think" about his response and prioritize the three most important things in life that he valued. The following week his wife was much better, and his response still did not change. Music was number one and his wife a close second. I revealed a pensive smile and he inquired what did I value most in life; wasn't it music…? I simply said, "No… music is number three on my list" (see Chapter Seven, *Role Model*). What I valued most in life was health first and foremost, family second, and finally music. He was perplexed and still didn't get it. I said, "You will." Time ran out again. The next lesson he came in beaming… "You're right!" I'm not quite sure what epiphany he had but those thought-provoking exchanges in his lessons and his self-realization of what he valued most in life gave me the deepest satisfaction of helping to guide him to an invaluable life lesson that will serve him well beyond any complicated percussion etude I could have exposed him to.

Webster's defines compassion as "deep awareness of the suffering of another coupled with the wish to relieve it" – from the Latin, it means literally "suffering with." While I do not equate suffering with teaching or learning, your students' struggles are plainly visible to you throughout their education. It is your duty to intervene, when appropriate, and to help your students through a crisis in their educational house or elsewhere. The sensitivity that you have developed in the classroom, coupled with your own life experience, will guide you in knowing when and how to compassionately intercede in order to best help your students.

From his book *The End of Education*, Neil Postman suggests that many of our most vexing and painful social problems could be ameliorated if we knew how to school our young; and yet, not much of our "education" takes place in school. He states, "At its best schooling can be about how to make a life, which is quite different from how to make a living." Learning is part of life, and life is all about learning. You cannot arbitrarily decide when the learning starts and life begins, or when life begins and the learning starts. Both are tightly wrapped around one another. Your constant exposure to young minds in the classroom reminds you of your responsibility at all times for guiding your students to learn not just about music, but about life.

In his new book *Overcoming Life's Disappointments*, Rabbi Harold Kushner shares similar sentiments: "You will read a magazine article about someone who came from the most unpromising of circumstances – inner city ghetto, crime, and drugs all around, absent father – and he or she went on to become a success and a role model, an outstanding athlete, a doctor or a nurse, an effective politician. The interviewer will ask how did you do it? And the answer will always begin with the same four words: 'There was this teacher.'"

Particular students can leave an indelible mark on you as a teacher, and frequently this has little to do with what you teach. Several weeks ago I received a phone call from a student who said I might not remember him from the late '90s; he said his name was PJ. And of course I knew instantly who he was... he always wore a Columbo-like trench coat. The trench coat was long gone, he laughed, but he was flattered I remembered him (in fact he was one of my favorite students). But I was more flattered that he remembered me, and wanted to turn to me for support. PJ was experiencing some difficult transitional life events, and sought me out for advice to redirect and refocus his music and his life. As Rabbi Kushner reminds us, "There was this teacher..."

If you find yourself cultivating a friendship with a student, it is best to wait until after graduation to pursue it deeply. That is not to say that a cup of coffee outside the classroom will do any harm. This sort of innocuous social interaction is entirely acceptable, but anything more than simple activities and conversation outside of the academic realm can put a great strain on the delicate thread of mentoring.

From time to time students extend invitations to have a beer and socialize. I am adamant not to accept an offer like this until that particular student has successfully graduated. Then, as a sort of "rite of passage," I in turn invite them for a six-mile fun run on the Boston marathon course – a section that includes

FRIENDSHIP

the famous Heartbreak Hill – before we grab that beer or sit down to dinner. This activity allows the natural boundaries of the classroom to disintegrate and a new "life relationship" to take seed.

Why create an additional burden on your thoughts when attempting to remain pure, objective, and honest in order to be fair to all students? You must remember at all times that one of your main objectives as teachers is to continually evaluate students, and this requires impartiality across the board. After graduation, any artificial boundaries that are in place between teacher and student can easily be erased. And it is much easier to have those boundaries in place well before any misjudgment occurs than to try to reconstruct them later. (And to be clear, I am not discussing romantic involvement; it goes without saying that any romantic involvement between a teacher and a student is totally unacceptable at any time.)

There will also come a time in each teacher's career when his students might surpass him. It is inevitable, and happens for a variety of reasons. The reasons themselves are unimportant. What is important is that you accept this natural transition with the grace befitting your profession. Some of your biggest life fulfillments and delights should lie with your students' own accomplishments. Such success validates your teaching principles. They will draw other students to you. And, most importantly, your best students are the ones who are the most fertile seeds of the next generation of educators. Insecure thoughts about a student's accomplishments have no place in your educational temple. Rather, a student's achievements should be celebrated by both teacher and student and should serve as inspiration to fellow students and an example of all that is possible.

Wisdom and experience come with age. Youth will never catch age. And even if your performance skills decline ever so slightly (as they invariably do), the richness of who you are as a teacher will only ripen with time. Time is your friend and ally in the classroom like it is in no other setting; slowly but surely, it makes us better teachers. Banner and Cannon succinctly conclude: "The wonders and satisfaction of teaching result from our ongoing ability to call up our knowledge of life from our own inner store of understanding for the good of those we are trying to teach." May aging take your speed if it increases that store.

Chapter Ten

TECHNIQUES FOR CREATIVE TEACHING

"Music is playing with silence."
~ Barry Harris

Hard Of Hearing: I often say, "I couldn't hear what you said; could you repeat that?" Literally, this may very well be true. But this can be a very effective technique to get the students to hear their *own* words, which they will carry with themselves far longer than anything you say. It is a very powerful tool to reverse negative thought patterns when a student is constantly down on their musical abilities. When a student says, "That wasn't as bad as I thought," or "I played pretty good!" or "They liked my playing," this is a moment you should seize upon – these self-made compliments are WORTH REPEATING!

I Forget: "Can you remind me, help me out?" Spoken by the teacher, this disarms the student. These few words humanize the teacher, and take the pressure off of a student who's afraid to give a wrong answer. Forgetfulness is "okay" if it is not a repeated pattern. Turning to the class for help remembering something will encourage students who may have been disinterested or afraid to volunteer an answer and engage more students to participate in class discussion. It also demonstrates your fallibility. More importantly, it suggests that there are always more solutions/ answers to any given question than merely the "correct" response.

Red Light, Green Light; "Don't Stop...": This is a vital technique that allows you to talk to a student as they are in the process of doing something, like working on hand position, body motion, or posture. This catches them in the *process*, and has greater impact on the correction... they witness the actual change take place ... they see it and *feel* it as you direct the adjustment. "Don't stop" lets you talk while they continue to play. This is very important, because the *moment* of what you are correcting will be lost if the student cannot actually witness the behavior you seek to correct. The sense of *feel* can be directly addressed only in the moment. "What you are doing NOW is incorrect, change it; now *this* is what it feels like to be correct. Can you feel and see the difference?" This lesson would lose its power completely if the student stopped what he was doing.

The Samie Experiment: When I was a student under Alan Dawson, he explained to me that sometimes he would read the newspaper and practice a long exercise called *The Ritual* simultaneously. Initially, this intentional double tasking bothered me. I am a firm believer in the "one mind, one focus" Zen approach: whatever it is we are doing, we should be fully engaged in it, without distraction. Years later, after my thinking had expanded and I had begun teaching, I was trying to guide an excellent student through a specific exercise that he was having great difficulty playing. I was willing to take a gamble with this particular student, because nothing conventional would solve this problem. I never tried Alan's disassociate approach or "muscle memory" technique before, and this seemed like the perfect opportunity.

Samie was a great student, diligent in his practicing, and he had excellent hand technique. I was attempting to isolate his right hand with cymbal patterns, and get him to play with fast, up-tempo CDs. This is a technique I frequently use with students, to great effect. If done correctly, this exercise accomplishes several goals:

> A) It allows the student to focus strictly on one limb in his

TECHNIQUES FOR CREATIVE TEACHING

    drumming – in this case, the right hand, the most important limb in jazz drumming.

B) It allows the student to play along with the "Masters" (Tony Williams, Jimmy Cobb, etc.) and duplicate their sound and rhythm as best he can, to mimic the exact patterns the Masters are playing without being distracted by three other limbs.

C) It is also an endurance builder – it goes on for 20 minutes, building strength in the wrist and fingers.

Samie's problem was not that he couldn't perform this exercise – he could do it, but everything he played for me sounded tense and forced, without any relaxation. He was trying too hard. So I suggested that he play along to the record once in the morning (just as we'd originally discussed), then try it once at night. The second time though, he was to try reading something, at the same time, so that the actual music would be secondary or in the background. My hope was that if he thought less about what he was doing it would become easier to do. It worked beautifully.

As teachers you must be a constantly evolving with your students. You must have the sensitivity, willingness, and openness to recognize the moment when it is necessary to abandon a technique that is "proven" but doesn't work for a specific student who needs a different approach. You may have used a technique for years, always finding it extremely effective. However, when confronted with less than the desired results with a particular student, you must be willing to go beyond what has been successful in the past and be open to any possibility that may help him succeed in the present.

Know Thy Instrument: A big part of my teaching revolves around constructing solos and original compositions for drums. Most students today may be fairly proficient, but they still do not *know* their instruments. They could play even better if they

RHYTHMIC REFLECTIONS ON CREATIVE TEACHING

truly knew their instruments. The isolation of the drum set as a solo compositional voice can be frightening. It is very easy to be on stage surrounded by other musicians, but to be alone for an entire solo concert can be tremendously intimidating, and having something to say musically is very difficult. When I assign a solo piece, I intentionally give few guidelines. When my students come in to class to play, I invariably get the following comments:

1) "I didn't know what to play."

2) "I never thought about a drum composition like that before."

Already, the assignment has succeeded! For perhaps the first time, they actually *thought* about their instrument and its possibilities. If I never hear them play a note, I know at least they are starting to recognize their instrument and all its capabilities, and they will be better off for starting to develop that intimacy with their instrument. Though the students might not appreciate the significance of the solo assignment right away, they come to discover that it is not the solo itself, but the experience of thinking about the solo that is the most valuable component.

When a five year-old asks about God in Unitarianism, the Unitarian's approach is to explain what they think are all the possibilities about God, not to answer the question directly. They then encourage the five year-old to join the dialogue by asking, "What do *you* think?"

The same premise applies in solo construction: it's not the answer that counts, but the thought process. In other words, the lack of an answer is the answer itself. Solo construction stimulates imagination, spontaneity, and creativity, and it emphasizes that all things are possible and worth thinking about. It also validates the benefits you can reap by exploring uncharted waters.

Thumbs Up: This universally familiar sign does not

interfere with the student's performance. It signals immediate approval and explicitly tells the student that he is performing the technique or piece correctly. Voice interference will always distract the student or halt their playing, so unless that's your intention, don't interject any verbal comment.

The "Skip Note": (*specifically related to drummers*) The skip note is smaller in sound and less important than other notes. However, if the timing of it is off, it can disrupt all the quarter notes that follow. The lack of its own importance creates its importance.

By Demonstration: In any private lesson or class, let the student self-correct, criticize, and substantiate his own performance before volunteering your own critique. A student's own words are retained far longer than yours.

Student Before Teacher: You must relate to students on their level first before they trust you, or fully relate to the subsequent information you give them. The first interview in class is essential to establishing students' background, influences, and idols. This will allow you to make individual references to each student when you make an analogy or correction. The student will more easily identify with what you are saying if you make a good-faith effort to connect with him on a personal level. Learning your student's backgrounds and influences also demonstrates your interest in them as individuals. They will respect you and relate to you better.

The Real Deal: Always attempt to create an actual performance when making a demonstration to your students (in other words, make them visualize it). The impact will be far greater. If a drummer is playing too loudly, gently suggest: "Remember – the vocalist forgot her microphone." Even as a hypothetical, this immediately calls the drummer's attention to the sound dynamics. Moreover, it effectively sensitizes students to a scary situation they might actually encounter onstage (no matter how remote the possibility), and teaches them how to react without getting thrown off center.

Each One Teach One: At all times, let students correct one another. They are more receptive to each other's comments, and it keeps the class and performer involved with one another.

Never A Dumb Question: Many times students are afraid to ask a question for fear it will be considered "dumb." You should strongly admonish them that the really "dumb" part is never asking the question!

Indirect Is The Most Direct: In ensembles there is usually very little eye contact in the beginning part of the semester. Students rarely look at one another and yet it is impossible to perform well as an ensemble without maintaining eye contact. To stress the point, you could do one of two things. Have each student face an opposite wall and then direct them to play a tune together or, start a simple conversation with one of them, but with your back turned so that you are talking into space. Either approach is extremely effective without you having to tell them directly that they need to be looking at each other.

"1, 2; 1, 2, 3, 4": One of the simplest yet most overlooked skills in developing leadership is counting off a tune. It not only allows all of the performers to start together, it instills in them a *feel* for the tune before they play one note. Although there are no special techniques involved in the count, it is the "doing it" that perpetuates the doing. Most issues such as visual contact, time signatures, groove/style considerations, and melody can be explored and resolved through this approach.

"Hi! How Are You?": The human voice is our original instrument; but it can become under-utilized and almost forgotten if you dedicate yourselves fully to another instrument. If you cannot *sing* a musical phrase, you will not be able to play it. To make that connection, one suggestion is to have students from different countries speak a welcoming gesture in their native language, then have a different student play the *shape* and *sound* of that phrase, and make a motivic solo out of it. This exercise broadens students' perspectives, and forces them to think outside the box about everything that is possible in constructing a solo. It encourages them to think from another instrument's perspective. Moreover, it naturally helps to integrate a multicultural class into a respectful, harmonic whole.

By Example: Observation is a key factor in learning. To demonstrate a point through a performance, I will ask the student to play a solo, and then I will play a solo based on the same tune. I then ask him if he remembers what he played during a particular section of the tune. Usually, the student can't recall. I then ask him if he remembers what I played, having intentionally left an entire section (usually the bridge, or B section) filled with rests. The student always remembers what I played – or, in this case, didn't play. I am quick to remind him, that he played many different combinations of notes and yet cannot remember one of them, and I didn't play one note and he remembered it clearly. This is often the first time a student remembers "nothing" as "something."

What Is It?: When a student fails to use a particular piece of the drum set, and probably should have (for example, the crash cymbal), rather than asking why he didn't use it, I disarmingly point and ask, "What do you call this...?" Calling attention to its exclusion without naming it or its purpose puts greater focus on its inclusion next time around.

Isolation: In private lessons I concentrate on the ride cymbal, the most important element of the drum set in jazz. Recently I had a student play for me, and everything was too loud. His focus had left the ride cymbal, so I told him not to play the other three limbs, and just to concentrate on the ride cymbal... after two or three minutes, I said, "You may introduce your other limbs again," and within a half a second he played about five or six notes between bass drum and snare. I yelled out, "Oh! Making up for lost time?" and he got a big grin on his face. Just because he could use his other limbs didn't mean he *had* to... and if he played those notes so soon, it meant that they didn't mean anything. This is an excellent approach to demonstrate and impress upon a student the importance of "less is more." One note with meaning is better than five or six without!

"I Can't Count": Chart reading is a difficult component for ALL musicians to master. Students are initially very lazy and do not count measures in music. Sometimes, I'll have a student play a chart with a lot of odd phrasing and an irregular number of measures to count. I then stop the music somewhere in the middle of the chart (knowing where I am) and tell him, "I am lost; can you tell me where we are?" This disarms him, and allows you to stress the point of counting. You also get to check and see if the student himself is lost, or whether he was counting properly.

What You See Is What You Get: You should suggest to students that they practice in front of a mirror to self-correct certain problems. For example, biting your lip suggests tension, and slouching indicates bad posture that inhibits breathing and relaxation, yet many times students are totally unaware that they are doing these things. Observing a bad habit daily makes it easier to correct.

A Second Chance: In one class of mine, at midterm, I have the students sight-read an etude as part of the exam. I de-emphasize this as a major component of the test, telling them that it just allows me to pinpoint their direction for the second half of the semester. (This section of the test also allows me to reward a good student who can actually sight-read with some extra credit on the exam.) The bigger issue at stake – and my real purpose in administering this portion of the test – is that two weeks later, I pass out the sight-reading example in class and go over it in depth. Unknown to them, I will retest them the following week on the same piece. I am extremely hard on students who do not work on a piece when given an additional opportunity; invariably, several students will

TECHNIQUES FOR CREATIVE TEACHING

play the sight-reading test the second time around just as poorly as they did on the midterm. This prompts me to launch into my lecture that in music, and in life, it is very, very rare to have a second chance, and if you are given one, you should not squander it!

What You Hear Is Not What You Hear: Students generally overplay. Sensitivity toward what to play and when to play it slowly evolves with musical maturity, experience, and simple trial and error. By focusing on other instruments, students develop a greater sensitivity to those instruments, and their function within the ensemble. How can you accomplish this? You should have students transcribe the comping rhythms of guitar and piano. Specifically, this exercise helps them to identify where and when other instruments play accents ("resolution points") within musical phrases. Subliminally, this exercise affects many areas of their playing. It helps them to identify what resolution points are, and how their placement affects "the swing" in jazz. It also conditions them to listen beyond their own instrument and relate to and interact with the other instruments that form the rhythm family.

Right Or Wrong: You should emphasize to a student that there is not a right way or a wrong way to do something. The only constant is that there is always a consequence to their choice.

Early To Bed Early To Rise: An early office hour demonstrates that those who truly want to improve, seek help, and have the strongest desires to succeed, will make the effort at any time to seek further knowledge and guidance. Exceptions are always honored for the late night working student, family responsibilities, and long-distance commuters. However, there's no reason knowledge should be convenient for the lazy and uncommitted student.

Balance: Honor what a student wants, balanced with what they need.

The Exception Is The Rule: If you make an exception for one student, you need to make it available to all students.

RHYTHMIC REFLECTIONS ON CREATIVE TEACHING

Opposites Attract: Practice the opposite of what you are trying to achieve. Soft vs. loud, slow vs. fast, fewer notes vs. more notes, shorter phrases vs. longer phrases, staccato vs. legato. Strive for balance in your playing, and your playing will become more complete.

There Is Only One You: It becomes increasingly difficult to sound unique in music. Yet your *own* uniqueness is all you have, and individual expression often goes under-appreciated. Developing one's sound or one's own musical voice is essential to success. You should be adamant to all students that to play differently, you must think differently. Reframe your suggestions from another instrument's perspective. To short-circuit a particular entrenched habit or "lick," you can create an environment or approach that forces the student to perform in a very unlearned way. For a drummer, you might make them play with three sticks, two brushes, and a mallet in one hand and nothing in the other. You might have them play left-handed or one hand at a time. When you force these conditions, the student will be fresher in their approach because they do not have a defined pattern of motion or muscle memory to guide their music.

Honor Thy Self: As part of an exam, I often ask a student to pick what gives them the most trouble. If they play it with ease, then they were not forthright with me and I say that I cannot help them if they will not identify their own weaknesses. Done properly, this test reinforces what they need help with the most and defuses the testing atmosphere: "I want to hear what you can't play!" Done without judgment, this is a great technique for finding out what the class as a whole has the greatest difficulty with, and it allows you to concentrate specifically in the next meeting on examples that everyone found troubling.

What Color Is It?: Have you ever asked a student to spontaneously compose a solo, a collage, or a short story, based only on a color? It sounds bizarre, but this technique forces the student to move outside their comfort zone and exposes them to a fresh perspective. Imagine the possibilities in music when a solo is based on something completely abstract! Students naturally ponder color's subjectivity and multiple interpretations, and question the intent of a composer who finds inspiration in something so broad and intangible. It also introduces them to colors and shadings as possibilities for solo composition – ideas that should become an integral part of their musical landscape. It demonstrates to students that a solo can still be compelling and beautiful when they free themselves from convention and abandon their over-reliance on notes, chords, and scales as the only approach to structure and content.

A Future Teacher?: In one of my classes I will have students memorize a particular exercise. I then ask for a volunteer to come up and lead the class. When no one volunteers, I usually pick a student whom I feel will benefit the most from it – this might be a pupil with poor hands, or a lack of confidence. I then make it a point to sit with the other students, as a student. I take great care in helping the student I selected make it through the exercise. It is not important if they cannot play the exercise well. The importance lies in having the student sit in front of the class, lead his peers, and gain confidence in the "doing of it." Regardless of the quality of the performance, I ALWAYS make sure the entire class applauds loudly and supportively for their peer. Support the effort, not the outcome.

Ask The Question: I often assign small, supplemental reading assignments outside of class. The next class I inquire if there are any questions. Most often, there are none. Disappointed, I then ask them the questions I was hoping for. This allows me to discuss the pertinent information from the assigned reading, and observe if they actually did the assignment.

These techniques are mostly drum-specific. My approaches are directly related to my instrument and the language used in teaching drum set. Any of these techniques may be substituted for other instruments, musical settings, and life's own unique melody.

Chapter Eleven

"ZEN THOUGHTS FROM MY TEACHING"

"A blow is a gift."

~ Aikido saying

Sometimes what we see is not what we are looking at.

═══

There is no discipline involved in doing something that you love. The discipline comes when you no longer love doing it as much as you use to, yet you still do it.

═══

In performance, awareness to realize something creates the ability to change, as you become aware of it.

═══

Practice in a manner in which you would never play, and your playing will improve.

═══

RHYTHMIC REFLECTIONS ON CREATIVE TEACHING

Never ask a question you want an answer to; rather, strongly hint at everything that surrounds the question, and the student will forever remember the answer to the question you never asked.

Every answer has a question, but not every question has an answer.

If you stop having fun playing music, you should stop playing music.

Don't change what you are doing; change the way you *think* about what you are doing.

It is better to have an effect on one student than contact with 10.

A student always shows greater interest when they are closest to failing ... when the greatest interest should have been when they were succeeding.

Have minimal amount of contact, for maximum amount of sound.

If you can't hear what you are playing, how can you play what you hear?

"ZEN THOUGHTS FROM MY TEACHING"

You cannot tell a student *why* they should practice. You can only tell them *how* to practice.

Poor students always take care of themselves.

A student cannot move forward by looking forward.

Play something that has not been played before... then play it in a different way, then play it in a different place, then play it in a different way *again* – and if all of that is not possible, then at least play that "something" as if it were the first time you have ever played it.

Popularity should not validate the content of what you teach.

Who and what you are, are inseparable from what and how you teach. Ideally you should teach as you live, by example.

At any moment, a particular question and answer may change. A change in the moment will change both the question, and the answer.

Never do something that someone tells you to do, without knowing the reasons for doing it.

RHYTHMIC REFLECTIONS ON CREATIVE TEACHING

Choose *not* to play something – but not because you cannot play it!

Better to see and not say, then to say and not see.

Do it from yourself, not for yourself.

It's important to be able to reproduce the same sound before attempting to change that sound, otherwise you will not have a point of reference.

The first step to success is admitting failure.

The doing it perpetuates the doing.

Don't look so hard at what makes you different, but look at how you have done things differently.

Never doubt that you may have knowledge to share with a student who knows many things. There are many things he does not know, and that is what you must know.

Chapter Twelve

CELL PHONE and iPOD GENERATION

"There is more to life than increasing its speed."
~ Mahatma Gandhi

We are all creatures of habit, and when things are pleasurable or immersing for us, exposure to them fuels a potential addiction. I do not own a cell phone or have Internet access at home (both by choice), though I do own an iPod Nano. Today, virtually every student I know carries a smart phone, is online or texting far too much, and gets mesmerized by the latest uploads to YouTube. To an outside observer, these students are good candidates to enter a 12-step program on how to break their chronic texting and e-mail addiction. A recent study by the American Academy of Pediatrics is warning parents about "Facebook depression" and the twisted view the Internet can give young people about what is really happening around them. Facebook and Twitter invade every aspect of our lives, and "real-time connectivity" can be found in every student's pocket or backpack. But is all this technology making life any easier? Better to heed the timeless wisdom of Thoreau: "Simplify, simplify, simplify."

A student recently whispered to me, "Rumor has it that you do not have a cell phone…" and I said, "True." The student continued, "and they say you don't have Internet at home," and I smiled and said, "That is true, too." Totally perplexed by my nonchalance and zero interest to own any instantaneous, must-stay-in-touch tech gadgets, he ended with "That's deep…" I couldn't help but smile.

RHYTHMIC REFLECTIONS ON CREATIVE TEACHING

I am reluctant to change for change's sake. I attempt to keep an open mind to any possibilities that may improve my approach to educating young minds and the content I use to do it. And at this point, I have more questions about the benefits of technology in the classroom than I do answers.

Neil Postman aptly states, "All technological change is a Faustian bargain. For every advantage a new technology offers, there is always a corresponding disadvantage." I've sat in on piano classes with eight students sitting at electric/synth pianos; how do we discuss the sense of touch, dynamics, and pedal control when the instrument in front of us is not real? One is already painfully aware of the Broadway scenario with entire orchestras being replaced by two synthesizer players, and yet we are culpable, and bear responsibility for teaching those same individuals.

The introduction of the calculator diluted our ability to add, subtract, multiply, and divide. Did you ever give a cashier an amount greater then the total only to watch them struggle to give you the correct amount in return, wholly reliant on the "change due" figure displayed on their register? The typewriter destroyed cursive writing. Attention Deficit Disorder (ADD) is a relatively new medical diagnosis, and now it's nurtured around the clock by Twitter and YouTube. And GPS *"should be"* the great savior for our lost sense of (cultural) direction, but where are we headed? If we continually find ways to circumvent the development of creative thinking and seek shortcuts to solve every problem, we sacrifice the natural flow and deliberate rhythm of the world around us. The more that technology creeps into our lives, the higher a price we pay for our complicity and homogenization.

The amount of information now available to young minds is overwhelming, and they are becoming far too complacent in the face of this information. In general, young people exposed to the depths of the Internet are giving little thought to what they're being presented, and digesting new material slowly and superficially. Things like simple research and the act of reading a book are becoming archaic, vanishing at the press of a button. The new

CELL PHONE AND IPOD GENERATION

research button is Google or Wikipedia. The new book is the Kindle or the Nook, thin electronic tablets which can hold up to 1,000 e-books. Libraries are fast becoming a place for free high-speed Internet access, not hard-copy research. Thankfully, the modern library still remains a guaranteed sanctuary of quiet solitude from the continued onslaught of "cell phone interruptus." Perhaps that may be the predominant reason to go, just for the privacy and solitude.

Cyber indigestion and ADD/ADHD are the new maladies of this generation. May the Luddite revolution find its voice again! There is a reason yoga and meditation are being offered for the first time at the lower grade levels: realizing that they are growing up into a hectic world, children are requesting and responding to structured periods of quiet time and meditation as part of their daily school schedule. Business classes and MBA candidates are meditating five minutes as part of class/lecture time to establish a habit for their future stressed-filled lives. These developments are all relatively new, so research is incomplete, but so far the experiments are working. Once students get exposed meditation, they request that it become a daily part of regular class time – and this holds true across a whole range of age group levels.

Canadian scholar Marshal McLuhan once said, "How does the structure of a medium alter the ways in which people sense the world?" How many times have we read about a love affair ending with an impersonal text message, or a full-time job being ripped away from an employee via e-mail? We are losing touch with basic human skills and emotions that are vital to our very existence and ability to communicate in a genuine manner. How do we judge speed of delivery, intonation, emotion, and body gestures via e-mail? If we alter the basic structures of how we communicate at the simplest levels, face to face, what dire consequences will that have on a larger scale for a larger audience?

A CD burner in every classroom is not progress, it's convenience. What message are we sending to our students? The famous jazz saxophonist Joe Henderson remarked, "In my day we went out and bought the record to transcribe the solo... we would just drop the needle over and over again. Now you can buy the same solo off the Internet!" Students now can hit "shuffle" on their iPods, or, worse, "random play," which means they listen to each composition once before it disappears and reshuffles into the playlist, destined to reappear only 50 or 100 tunes later. How can students absorb and learn something that is gone in a cyber-second? In fact, students rarely buy entire CDs anymore; they just burn them, or worse, download one tune at a time. Don't they lose sense of the album as a whole, failing to grasp the cohesive concept the artists envisioned? And what does it mean that they give no credit to the process of musical creation, and never even learn about the equipment used, the inspiration for the album, or the personnel behind the recording?

I recently asked a student to play brushes, performing to a ballad of his choice. He came in and played along to a very stiff digitalized solo piano version of the Errol Garner classic *Misty*. It was horrible! He played like it sounded. And to make matters worse, he didn't even know who composed the tune! I asked how and more importantly why he had picked this particular selection. He said plainly, "I Googled 'ballads.'" His next assignment was to find and play along with the original.

Another time with a similar assignment a student came in and played a fairly nice version of *Nardis*, a jazz standard frequently played and made famous by pianist Bill Evans. I asked this student how he found the selection, and he said it was the next selection on his iPod. I smiled and asked (I knew I had him!) who was the drummer. He didn't know. His next assignment was to compile a brief history of *all* of Bill Evans's drummers, the time periods, and recordings that they were a part of – without simply citing the web!

I strongly encourage students to take handwritten notes. Recently after meeting with a new student, I told him what books and CDs I wanted him to buy. He began searching through his bag, and I was pleased to see that he planned to write down the appropriate information. But to my dismay (and, in truth, amusement), he took out his iPhone and promptly took pictures of all the books and CDs I'd recommended.

CELL PHONE AND IPOD GENERATION

Note taking is archaic. Cursive writing is nearing extinction. You would be hard pressed to find penmanship being taught as a subject in lower grade levels. And if you cannot write it, will you be able to read it? In the aftermath of Hurricane Katrina, New Orleans lost power and doctors had to write prescriptions and orders by hand. Imagine what would have happened if doctors forgot how to write scripts by hand, or nurses were so dependent on electronic medical records that manual instructions and prescriptions were like Greek to them? This might sound whimsical now, but something like it could be a reality in a generation or two.

A person's handwriting (or lack of it) is a window into their creative mind. It's as distinct as their voice, as unique to them as their laugh or giggle. As musicians/artists we are in a constant quest to find our own unique voice, to say something that has not been said before. If we lose our ability to read and write, the wonderful spontaneity of face-to-face conversation will soon follow. Texting is a sad case study in how true interaction is already being weakened. I believe it is severely stunting the emotional growth of our youth, and that this technological "convenience" comes at great expense to meaningful interpersonal experience.

Technology is increasingly invading our classrooms. Sadly, there is a greater reliance now on technical, time-optimizing solutions rather than reflection and critical judgment. In his book *The End of Education*, Neil Postman inquires, "Will speed of response become more than ever a defining quality of intelligence? Is virtual reality a new form of therapy?" Technology has evolved far too rapidly for us to healthfully digest. Consider the evolution process and the natural growth of man, and his adaptation to surroundings. This took us hundreds of years, and yet in less then five decades we've gone from the moon to a computer in every home, a phone in every car, to e-mail, to the Internet, to GPS, to virtual reality, to Facebook, to texting, to "OMG!"

I thought the arts, in their purity, would remain impervious to such influences and conflicts. I suppose they have, to some extent. Postman suggests, "The advantages and disadvantages of new technologies are never distributed evenly among the population. This means that every new technology benefits some and harms others." Does that mean that a computer in every classroom at MIT is more acceptable and necessary than a computer at Massachusetts College of Art and Design?

Postman continues: "Technology change is not additive: it is **ecological**, a new technology does not merely add something: it changes everything." If there is a place for technology in the classroom, I am not sure where that place is. We cannot ignore new technologies and must, it seems, explore ways to integrate them into the learning environment, but we must proceed cautiously. As educators, we cannot risk overwhelming our students, and must take care not to sacrifice the true beauty of learning and self-discovery.

Recently I was running behind and in a rush to get to class. I had my master cassette tape (first mistake) but could not find another tape of multiple examples of the same composition. When I started class and took out the master cassette tape, the class erupted in a unison – the mere site of a cassette was hilarious to them. A lone voice from the back of the room drove the knife in deeper: "You probably still have an eight track in your car!" I couldn't help but crack up too. Apologetically, I explained I couldn't find my recording with multiple versions of the Max Roach composition *The Drum Also Waltzes*, our lesson for the day. A student said "Just a second…" and within moments had found eleven different versions of the composition available on the web, most of which I didn't even know existed. I immediately assigned *all* of the versions to the class, including myself, and said we would discuss and compare each version to the original in the next session. In this case, a mild twist of fate allowed technology to creep into my classroom, and for this one time it worked and I was grateful.

The flip side occurs too, for which I am less grateful. This semester I was teaching my advanced brush lab and a student started to film my demonstration on his iPhone. This was a new experience for me. He didn't even ask permission to film me, which I promptly would have said no to. I calmly told him to stop and stay after class. He was embarrassed and deeply apologetic. I said it was flattering that he would want to record my lesson, and encouraging that he might want to review it again later, but filming someone is invasive and – particularly in a classroom – if you're focused on your recording device, you cannot truly be learning. You must live in the moment, rather than try to capture it for eternity.

As Gandhi said in the quote I used to open this chapter: "There is more to life than increasing its speed." To this I would add, there is more to education than increasing its speed as well. We should pay heed and not ignore the rhythm of the human heartbeat… It thumps *adagio*, or slowly. This is our own rhythm. Thoreau said to march to the beat of a different drummer. Although not the same context, the import of this instruction on today's society is clear. We must listen to our own heartbeat – we should dance with our own footsteps. We should embrace change, yes, but must remain hypersensitive to our motives and our methods. If technology can enrich our lives, then welcome it in, but be sure to question whether the sterile, impersonal shortcuts that new gadgets afford us are truly an improvement in the lives we lead today.

If there's one thing that technology cannot displace, it is the sanctity and meaning you gain from face-to-face interaction – and I don't mean teleconferencing on a webcam or using Skype. Nowhere is the value behind this interaction more compelling than between student and teacher. We need to listen and communicate in the presence of others, not online or via e-mail. The good news is, there is no replacing, speeding up, or processing out the *human element* involved with teaching! And if it ever is such a method, then we can no longer be teaching, nor can anyone really be learning. Of course, the virtual teacher and virtual classroom is now real… Or is it? Colleges across the country are embracing online teaching as a major source of revenue with almost no impact on campus resources or classroom space. From a budgeting perspective, it is the equivalent of "takeout" at a restaurant. Sarah Gold, who teaches an online class at University of California at Berkeley, remarked in a recent piece in *The New*

York Times, "I wouldn't know my students if I passed them on the street." Does this seem like something Ms. Gold is proud of...?

I will not teach an online course. This is not a statement of righteousness or stubbornness, nor do I fear the technologies that could make it possible. Quite simply, I believe online "teaching" robs the profession of everything most meaningful to it – interpersonal interaction, hands-on instruction, the proximity of teacher and student. And I feel this way for a reason. This past summer I had a former student travel all the way from India exclusively to study brushes with me. I was deeply honored and flattered that he would make such an intense effort to study alongside me. If he could have received my instruction over the web, without the nuisance and cost of travel, would he have elected this instead? Not a chance. There could be no mechanical substitute for our interactions. No portal on the web could have captured the fine points of our lessons together, or enabled the same depth of teacher/student relationship that we enjoy – and *that* is what this student came to Boston to experience again.

The difficulty with future education is not so much the acquisition of new knowledge, rather it is how we attempt to exchange and share our knowledge in a landscape that's changing all too quickly. Postman reminds us, "New technology is not about how to use it rather how it uses us!" New knowledge is never the problem, nor is technology itself, per se; you must instead consider the source, the intention, and the use of these new technologies. Does it really improve the teaching experience that you can send an e-mail instead of making an announcement in class? Are students learning more now that they have access to everything under the sun with "one click?" Can you convey meaning the same way through a webcam to a group of young people you've never met as you could if they were sitting in front of you every weekday? Technology might be knocking at your door, but you don't have to answer.

Chapter Thirteen

MUSIC AS THERAPY

*"Music produces a kind of pleasure which human nature
cannot do without…"*

~ Confucius

My initial exposure to the Music Therapy Department at Berklee was when I unceremoniously and literally stumbled into a colleague's studio with the lights dimly lit and a student lying on the floor surrounded by her peers in a circle, playing very large Native American drums, beating a trance-like hypnotic rhythm. I later found out the rhythm was appropriately called *heartbeat*. I immediately turned around and profusely apologized for my interruption and delicately retreated out the door. My mind began racing. What class was this? Whatever it is I want in! I impatiently waited until the class ended and "ceremoniously" barged in. This time, only my colleague remained. With a furtive grin he remarked, "I knew you would be back."

"Wha..clas…" "Music Therapy!" "What the hell were they doing?" "It's called a drum massage and we were playing a Native American rhythm called *Heartbeat*.." "May I take the class…?" "Sure, you can take the class AND we should definitely talk, because it's very possible that another section would be needed and you would be perfect to teach it. Are you interested?" I just smiled….

Ten years later my smile has grown bigger, just like the blossoming Music Therapy Department at Berklee and worldwide.

In fact, Music Therapy is becoming one of the fastest growing majors in the country and Berklee College is recognized as one of the leading colleges in research and development complementing and reflecting Boston as a medical "Mecca" for countless treatments of various life-threatening illnesses throughout the world.

The history of music therapy, its origins, and the earliest writings and documentation might be traced to the simple *genesis* of the very first sounds we ever hear in the acoustic chamber of the womb. And perhaps the very first *pure* sound we hear is that of our mother's heartbeat. For the rest of our life, our heartbeat will inform and dictate to us the rhythm of life. It will tell us when to relax, when to slow down, and when to push a little. It will enlighten us when we are out of rhythm with ourselves (or with others), and through it we will know when to go with the flow and move with the rhythm of the universe. In his book *The Tao of Physics*, Fritjof Capra states: "Rhythmic patterns appear throughout the universe, from the very small to the very large. Atoms are patterns of probability waves, molecules are vibrating structures, and living organisms manifest multiple, interdependent patterns of fluctuations. Plants, animals, and human beings undergo cycles of activity and rest, and their physiological functions oscillate in rhythms of various periodicities."

Scientific studies have also determined that there is a predisposition in the universe toward a complex harmonic phenomenon known as *entrainment*. Entrainment is "The process by which the powerful rhythmic vibrations of one object are projected upon a second object with a similar frequency, thereby causing that object to vibrate in resonance with the first object; In terms of the human organism, causing us to vibrate in resonance with those waves in a variety of interconnected ways." Doesn't this phenomenon take seed even before we are born?

Thrust into an unknown world, we arrive with our own voice screaming harmony with rhythm. Our eyes open or close with the help of eyelids, perhaps in a prelude to later life, when we choose not to see something we do not want to see. Minus the counterpoint of not having "ear lids," the symphony of life will continue without

MUSIC AS THERAPY

an intermission. That unique primal cry, like your family-coded DNA, will be your own original melody that your mother will always identify in a room of like-minded, cacophonous babies. She'll pick you up and put you next to her warm chest beating out that mesmerizing first rhythm you know so well... and start perhaps humming or singing a soft, soothing lullaby. Sufi master Hazrat Inayat Khan eloquently suggests something similar: "The physical effect of sound has also a great influence upon the human body. The whole mechanism, the muscles, the blood circulation, the nerves, are all moved by the power of vibration. As there is resonance for every sound, so the human body is a living resonator for sound. Every pitch that is a natural of the voice will be a source of a person's own healing as well as that of others when he sings a note of that pitch."

Konrad Lorenz, who was a Nobel Prize winner and a specialist in animal behavior, observed while studying ducklings newly hatched from eggs that the tiny animals waddled toward him as soon as they heard his voice. In another experiment, neurologist Andre Thomas assembled a group of adults and gathered them around an infant just 10 days after its birth. One after another, they spoke the child's newly-given name aloud... and there was no reaction or movement from the child until its own mother pronounced the name.

From his book *The Conscious Ear*, the French physician Alfred Tomatis states: "The fetus hears an entire range of predominantly low frequency sounds... the universe of sound in which the embryo is submerged is remarkably rich in sound qualities of every kind, and then the mother's voice asserts itself in this context, a noise in the form of a coded message of exceptional quality..." It is here that healing begins.

What is it about music that is inescapable? Why is it so omnipresent and continually flooding the air? According to Daniel Levitin, author of *This Is Your Brain on Music*, "When we listen to music, the levels of the brain chemicals dopamine and serotonin increase!" In fact, one of the Chinese characters for medicine is the same as the character for music, and the characters representing music and happiness are exactly the same!

Confucius also suggested that "Music produces a kind of pleasure that human nature cannot do without." In an article in *The Boston Globe*, archeologists in Germany unearthed a flute carved from bone and ivory that was 35,000 years old. Artistic expression was vital even to prehistoric man – in fact, prehistoric man could sing and dance centuries before structured speech evolved.

Mitchell Gaynor is a world famous oncologist who has integrated sound healing (particularly singing bowls) as part of his practice. In his incredible book *Sounds of Healing*, Gaynor describes the famous story of the previously mentioned French physician Alfred Tomatis, who has been recognized by the French Academy of Science and Medicine for his revolutionary research and clinical work in the area of hearing and sound. In the 1960s at a Benedictine monastery in southern France, many of the monks were suffering from a mysterious sickness. Fatigue and exhaustion plagued their normal workday, and conventional medicines were to no avail. One doctor suggested the vegetarian monks adopt a diet of eating meat, but this only made things worse. After much consultation and observation, Tomatis determined the cause of the illness. A young abbot who was a recent arrival to the monastery had directed the monks to abandon their six to eight hours of singing Gregorian chants each day, insisting that they devote more time to other practices. Convinced this abstinence was the problem, Tomatis recommended the monks immediately resume the practice of chanting, describing the chants as "energy food." Within five months after returning to their normal routine and chanting daily, the monks had fully recovered.

Music therapy is a relatively new field, though the concept has its roots in antiquity. The earliest references are the writings from the Bible in the first Book of Samuel, when King Saul was "overwhelmed by an evil spirit from the lord" and his servants counseled him to employ a harpist whose playing might heal and soothe his troubled soul. King Saul summoned David, a skilled harpist and musician whose artful playing made King Saul well again. It is no coincidence that in this

MUSIC AS THERAPY

passage, one of the first recorded moments of music therapy, the instrument used was the harp. With its oscillating strings with healing vibrations, the harp – along with the guitar – is one of the most popular instruments used in music therapy today.

Pythagoras, the famous Greek philosopher and mathematician, may be considered the first intellectual in this field and the "spiritual godfather" of sound medicine. He is credited as the first person to take an organized approach to using music as a healing technique. Gaynor cites Iamblichus, who studied the theories of Pythagoras, as noting the following: "Pythagoras considered that music contributed greatly to health if used in the right way. He called his method 'musical medicine.' In the spring he would sit in the middle of his disciples who were able to sing and play his lyre, and his followers would sing in unison certain chants or paeans by which they appeared to be delighted and became melodious and rhythmical. At other times his disciples also employed music as medicine with certain melodies composed to cure the passions of the psyche, as well as ones for despondency and mental anguish. In addition to these medical aids, there were other melodies for anger and aggression and for all psychic disturbances." In his book *Musicophilia*, Oliver Sacks references numerous case studies of patients who have experienced strokes, been afflicted with Parkinson's disease, or suffer from dementia and Alzheimer's who have responded remarkably well when music is introduced into their rehabilitation routine.

More recently there have been countless clinical studies emerging that show a positive link between music and physical and emotional recovery. Perhaps some of the most famous ones are documented in Don Campbell's *The Mozart Effect*, which describes the positive impact that certain kinds of music can have on plants and animals. If music has such a positive effect on plants and animals, it makes perfect sense that music can have a positive and healing effect on us!

One of my most pain-filled, depressing periods of my life was the end of my 17-year marriage. I have no doubt that my healing process was sustained and accelerated by music. The comfort and support of my family and friends gave me strength, but music filled a void that nothing else could. On the days I was emotionally paralyzed and felt unable to do anything, I played my drums for hours... I loved them and they loved me back, unconditionally. And on the days I didn't have the strength or desire to play the drums, I listened to music instead. I was my own "Music Therapist."

My continued exposure to music therapy comes through my friendship with Dr. Suzanne Hanser, who is the Chair of the Music Therapy Department at Berklee College. Using my experience and research, I now teach several classes and ensembles in the department. In these particular classes, I go around the room and ask each student if they had an epiphany in their decision to become a Music Therapist, and most have a personal story. They have a grandmother or father with Alzheimer's or Parkinson's, a special needs brother or sister, or a close relative who had a stroke. All of the students have the gift of music, and a deep personal connection that inspires them to pursue a life helping others with their music. I tell them I've had no personal epiphany similar to theirs, but having played music for so long I have countless times witnessed the power of music and I know its innate potential to heal....

I founded the Music Therapy Ensemble at Berklee. Part of the requirement is to give a concert at an off-campus venue, usually at an assisted living center or other facility where music can work its healing magic to greatest effect. Two years ago, we traveled to an assisted living facility for Alzheimer's patients to sing Christmas carols for the residents. Some were already in the large room in their hospital beds; others were in their wheelchairs. Most of the residents were catatonic or gazing into space. But when we started singing, the entire room came to life – literally every patient in the room started to sing along with us, recalling EVERY word. Our encore was "Silent Night." When we finished the encore, one patient raised their hand and asked if we knew Silent Night and would we sing it. A couple of us smiled and said yes, of course, and after we finished someone yelled out, "Do you know "Silent Night," it is my favorite Christmas carol," and I remarked it was our favorite too! We played it again for a third time, just as if it were the first. At the end, when we had to leave, tears were in all our eyes. The patients didn't want us to leave and we didn't want to leave. As we walked out, the residents slowly returned to their fixed gazes. It was heartrending. But we'd brought them comfort, sprinkled with loving joy, through music. Perhaps they even felt healed a little bit, in a world that only they know.

Music is a mystery to me. There is something about how profoundly it affects ALL of us that we may never fully understand. We each have a favorite song or a performer we love. How many times has a special song – one entwined with deep, poignant memories because we associate it with a time and a place – transported us back to a place of happiness, or melancholy, bringing tears to our eyes with the memory? Music is extremely powerful. It's a non-drug with narcotic consequences, and a whole host of hidden side effects. Of all the arts – painting, drama, poetry, writing, sculpting – music is perhaps the only one that affects us physically and viscerally. Imagine when we go to the Museum of Fine Arts and become captivated by a Monet painting. The work may be stunning, yes, but do we start moving around and gyrating? No, we remain still and transfixed. If we go to a poetry reading we sit motionless in our chairs… listening attentively, but unprovoked to do anything but sit quietly in contemplative reflection. And yet, if we go to a concert or put on the radio and music fills the air, most of us immediately start to move our feet, our arms, and soon our entire body is in motion. WHY? I don't exactly know. I only know that it works….

Chapter Fourteen

MENTORS

*"Preachers err by trying to talk people into belief;
better they reveal the
radiance of their own discovery."*

~ Joseph Campbell

Tony Monforte was my first drum teacher. From the age of 10 until I left to attend Northeastern University in Boston at age 18, Tony was my mentor. I continued to study privately with him while I attended Northeastern. Ultimately, Tony wrote me a letter of introduction to Alan Dawson, who was one of the founding "Drum Fathers" of the Berklee Percussion Department. I never realized the impact Tony had on me as a teacher until I started to teach. I remember the time Tony had to raise his fee, and my dad could not afford it. Tony said "Mr. Hazilla no problem; just have Little Jonnie put the usual amount in the drawer so the other students won't see." There are many lessons to be taken from that, beyond the obvious. The one I take to heart is money didn't matter to Tony… helping someone did. He cared. Ever the teacher/mentor, the greatest lesson of all was revealed at the end Chapter Five… "Never forget your roots, Little Jonnie H!" Tony reminds me yearly at his "Drumarama" that where you come from matters, and you should always respect those who helped you get where you are today.

Ran Blake was chair of the Third Stream Department at New England Conservatory in the 1980s. He sent a satellite group of students to Northeastern one afternoon to play for our Jazz Appreciation class. I was so taken with this jazz performance that I decided I no longer wanted to be a French major and join the Peace Corps. I set up an interview and audition with Ran. He mentioned in an excited tone that I would be the first drummer to enroll in his department. And I was equally enthusiastic. It was not so thrilling in my audition when Ran asked me to play, and I quote, "What Boston would sound like on a grey dark morning..." His only comment about my impromptu performance was it "sounded more like a Boston rush hour!" No one had ever asked me to play something like that. And more importantly, at the time, I didn't even think about music and drums in that way. Just as my students today wonder aloud, "How on earth can I play a *color*?" so too did I struggle with that first request for an abstract performance. Ran was the Zen Master... "the teacher appears when the student is ready!"

Ran assigned me so many projects that were not "drum friendly"... there was a time when I cursed him and wanted to leave school. He asked me to compose a solo piece for Olivier Messiaen's *Quartet for the End of Time*... the assignment was brilliant... my solo was not. But the seed was planted in me. One time while playing a duet on the jazz standard *Bye Bye Blackbird* Ran suggested I "think more like Miles Davis on muted trumpet." I didn't understand his meaning then, but I get it now.

Ran taught me the importance of critical listening and how to blend positive comments with negative ones so the performer would grasp both. Ran taught me loyalty and how important it was to support one another by attending concerts and recitals. Ran led by example – he still attends more student concerts then anyone I know. His insistence that I move to New York – "as all serious artists do" – was perhaps his most instructive gift. He said, "You have to go for at least two years, and stay no matter how bad it gets!" I went for two, stayed for eight, and it got pretty bad... but it was the best thing I could have ever done musically, and

I have Ran to thank for his careful, calculated, and loving push.

Bob Rusch is the founder of Cadence Records, the jazz label C.I.M.P., and "Cadence Magazine." Bob was the first producer to respond to my first trio recording and release it commercially. He subsequently released three more collections of my work, though he turned down two others. Bob is known in the recording industry as being brutally honest, and somewhat abrasive. He tells you things you don't necessarily want to hear, but they always ring true and resonate with integrity. Bob has mentored me when negotiating other recording contracts, even when to do so meant I would get a better deal elsewhere than he could offer. He has handed me a large check for royalties on a recording done many years before, guaranteed by a contract I had long ago forgotten. No one in the industry does that! He has released hundreds of recordings of obscure individuals because he liked the music and thought their artistic contribution was valuable and needed to be documented, knowing full well it was a losing financial proposition. He always paid his musicians on the spot, which was (and is) extremely rare. He taught me never to believe the good reviews because I would have to believe the bad ones as well... "So don't believe either."

Perhaps the most salient moment that revealed Bob's natural gift to record and produce was when I recorded my third CD for him, *Form and Function*. It was a radical departure from my comfort zone of leading a trio, and Bob once again gave me a chance when no one else would. The instrumentation was three saxophones, one trombone, and drums. All of the musicians were fellow faculty members at Berklee College of Music. After several repeated takes of one particular tune, which I thought were pretty good, Bob yelled out in exasperation: "You all sound like a bunch of academic teachers in a classroom. Jesus just play something that is not so GODDAMN PERFECT! Don't worry about what comes out, just let it come out!" It worked! The next take was a keeper. And so is Bob. He is as unique as the music he produces, and I would not be where I am now musically if it weren't for his support, mentoring, and honesty.

Joe Hunt was a senior member of the Percussion Department at Berklee when I was hired. Early on, we shared the same studio. This arrangement could not have been more fortuitous. With almost every problem I experienced in my green years, I went to Joe for his wise counsel. He had done it all and experienced it all, and not once did his advice mislead me – his words were spot on every time. When I encountered my first student who did not like me or my teaching approach and wanted to switch to another teacher, I was depressed and humiliated. How could someone dislike me that intensely, and worse, feel the need to rebel against my approach to teaching? I went to Joe and explained my conundrum. He wisely inquired how many private students I had. I said 22. He got a big smile on his face and said "Jon, one out of 22 isn't bad... and if you stick around, there will be a few more in your career too!" Ahhhh, instant relief – nothing more needed to be said.

Joe was one of my biggest supporters to obtain full-time status at the college. In fact, his vision for me was that I would be his replacement when he retired. That did not sit well with the department chair, and we both were in an awkward and uncomfortable environment for several years. When I tried to take the matter into my own hands, Joe wisely cautioned, "Don't buck rank!" And believe me, was he ever right! Joe finally retired and I eventually achieved full-time status as we'd both hoped – though not because of any foolish intervention I was planning. I still see Joe and we have lunch periodically. He has helped me in life issues as well. Joe's resiliency in life and music continue to inspire me and I'm deeply indebted to him for his continued guidance.

The Reverend Martha Niebanck is a co-minister at First Parish Unitarian Universalist church in Brookline, Massachusetts. I am a member of this church, and as my involvement within the spiritual community has deepened, so too has my connection with Rev. Martha. I was chair of the Caring Committee for three years, and Rev. Martha was the advisor. It's hard to put my finger on exactly how Rev. Martha continues to nurture and mentor my spiritual growth, but without her I would not have reached such a spiritually rich moment in my life. She never offers advice. Her wise, compassionate listening allows me to find and explore the questions that only I have the answer(s) to.

I was asked recently by the other co-minister, Rev. Jim Sherblom, to give a testimony to First Parish and answer the following question: "Why does a Berklee drumming professor embrace and devote such care to our Ministry?" The following is an excerpt of my response: "*I've been on the faculty at Berklee for 25 years. Every one of those 25 years still feels like my first... I have an undying passion for my vocation. I'm both lucky and forever grateful that I have found my true calling... or perhaps it found me. To care for others and always be willing to help is in my nature, and comes easily to me. But as with drumming, living a good life requires daily practice... I have found the best teachers are not the ones who know the most... but the ones who care the most. I strive to fit this mold.*

"*In his book* On Caring, *Milton Mayeroff states: 'In order to care I must understand the other's needs and I must be able to respond properly to them, and clearly good intentions do not guarantee this. To care for someone, I must know many things. I must know for example who the other is, what his powers and limitations are, what his needs are, and what is conducive to his growth. I must know how to respond to his needs, and what my own powers and limitations are.*'*

"*As my years of teaching at Berklee have unfolded I have discovered it's less about music and more about life... or the music in our life... I'm convinced of this more and more every day. This past Spring I had three former students (all from the late '90s) contact me. Each one wanted to get together with me... not for a drum lesson, but for coffee – to talk about the crossroads and struggles they are now confronting in life. I'm deeply flattered and honored that after so many years, they each sought me out...*

"*Perhaps what they remembered when they walked through my studio door was that I shook their hand and warmly welcomed them, from deep within my heart... that I asked them many questions... where they are from... why were they here? I asked what their dreams and goals were.... we never picked up a drumstick during that first lesson... we only talked. What they sensed was that I genuinely cared about them, and that my deep sense of responsibility would not end with their graduation ceremony...*"

My resolve and sense of responsibility has only deepened with Rev. Martha's love-filled mentoring. My ongoing spiritual quest coupled with her guidance has revealed to me, that spirituality, life, and music are inseparable, and collectively constitute who I have become....

"Those who seek mentoring will rule the great expanse under the heaven. Those who boast that they are greater than others will fall short. Those who are willing to learn from others, become greater. Those who are ego-involved will be humbled and made small."

~ Shu Ching

To all who have mentored me in big and small ways, to all of those I have mentored, and to all of those who are mentors and do not yet realize it....

Gasho!

* *This quote was previously referenced in the Introduction.*

Mosaic

All of us start with the same human frame. How we arrange the fragile pieces of glass, inside the frame... the different sizes, the many shapes, and endless unique patterns, is what makes us so different. And yet, they still are the same pieces of colored glass that we share and have in common... truly we could not be more different or more alike.

Bibliography

Banner, James & Harold C. Cannon. *The Elements Of Teaching*. New Haven: Yale Press, 1997.

Bolen, Jean Shinoda. *The Tao Of Psychology*. New York: Harper Collins, 1979.

Brandon, David. *Zen in the Art of Helping*. New York: Delta, 1976.

Bridges, William. *Transitions*. New York: Addison-Wesley, 1980.

Bruser, Madeline. *The Art Of Practicing*. New York: Bell Tower, 1997.

Cameron, Julia. *The Artist's Way*. New York: Tarcher Putnam, 1992.

Campbell, Joseph. *Reflections On The Art Of Living*. New York: Harper Collins, 1991.

Cardillo, Joseph. *Be Like Water*. New York: Warner Books, 2003.

Claremon, Neil. *Zen In Motion*. Rochester: Vermont Inner Traditions, 1991.

Cooper, Andrew. *Playing In The Zone*. Boston: Shambhala, 1998.

Covey, Stephen R. *The 7 Habits of Highly Effective People*. New York: Simon and Schuster, 1989.

Dass, Ram and Paul Gorman. *How Can I Help?* New York: Alfred A. Knopf, 1987.

Deshimaru, Taisen. *The Ring Of The Way*. New York: Dutton, 1983.

Draeger, Donn F. *Ninjutsu: The Art Of Invisiblity*. Rutland, Vermont: Tuttle Press, 1975.

Frankl, Victor. *Man's Search For Meaning*. New York: Washington Square Press, 1959.

BIBLIOGRAPHY

Gallwey, W. Timothy. *The Inner Game Of Tennis*. New York: Bantam, 1979.

Glassman, Bernie. *Infinite Circle*. Boston: Shambhala, 2002.

Gaynor, Mitchell. *Sounds of Healing*. New York: Broadway Books, 1999.

Gracian, Baltasar. *The Art Of Worldly Wisdom*. Trans. Joseph Jacobs. Boston: Shambhala Classics, 2000.

Heinrich, Bernd. *Why We Run*. New York: Ecco, 2001.

Herrigel, Eugen. *Zen In The Art of Archery*. New York: Vintage, 1953.

Herrigel, Gustie. *Zen In The Art Of Flower Arrangment*. Newton: Charles T. Branford Co., 1958.

Huang, Chungliang Al. *Thinking Body, Dancing Mind*. New York: Bantam, 1992.

Kapleau, Philip. *Straight To The Heart*. Boston: Shambhala, 2001.

Kiev, Ari. *A Strategy for Daily Living*. New York: Free Press, 1973.

Kiev, Ari. *A Strategy for Success*. NewYork: Social Psychiatry Research Institute, 1977.

Kim, Ashida. *Iron Body Ninja*. New York: Citadel Press, 1997.

Kushner, Harold S. *Overcoming Life's Disappointments*. New York: Anchor Books, 2006.

Langer, Ellen J. *On Becoming An Artist*. New York: Ballantine Books, 2005.

Langer, Ellen J. *The Power of Mindful Learning*. Reading: Addison-Wesley, 1997.

Lee, Bruce. *Tao of Jeet Kune Do*. Santa Clarita: Ohara Publications, 1975.

Lee, Bruce. *Striking Thoughts*. Rutland: Tuttle, 2000.

Loehr, James E. *Mental Toughness Training For Sports*. New York: Penguin, 1982.

Loori, John Daido. *The Zen Of Creativity*. New York: Ballantine, 2004.

Martin, Philip. *The Zen Path Through Depression*. San Francisco: Harper, 1999.

Mascetti, Mauela Dunn. *Sayings The Wisdom Of Zen*. New York: Hyperion, 1996.

McElheran, Brock. *Conducting Technique*. New York: Oxford Press, 1964.

Metcalf, Franz. *What Would The Buddha Do?* New York: Gramercy, 1999.

Millman, Dan. *Body Mind Mastery*. Novato: New World Library, 1999.

Musashi, Miyamoto. *The Book of Five Rings*. Boston: Shambhala, 1993.

Nachmanovitch, Steven. *Free Play Improvisation in Life and Art*. New York: Tarcher/Putnam, 1990.

Okakura, Kakuzo. *The Book Of Tea*. Boston: Shambhala Classics, 2001.

Orlick, Terry. *In Pursuit Of Excellence*. Champaign: Leisure Press, 1980.

Parcells, Bill. *Finding A Way To Win*. New York: Doubleday, 1995.

Pater, Robert. *The Black Belt Manager*. Rochester: Park Street Press, 1988.

Peale, Norman Vincent. *The Power of Positive Thinking*. New York: Fawcett, 1952.

Postman, Neil. *The End Of Education*. New York: Alfred Knopf, 1995.

Reps, Paul. *Zen Flesh Zen Bones*. New York: Anchor Press/Doubleday, 1930.

Reynolds, David. *Playing Ball on Running Water*. New York: Quill, 1984.

Roosevelt, Eleanor. *You Learn By Living*. Philadelphia: Westminster Press, 1960.

Salmon, Paul G. and Robert G. Meyer. *Notes From The Green Room*. New York: Lexington Books, 1992.

Schloegl, Irmgard. *The Wisdom Of The Zen Masters*. New York: New Directions, 1976.

Sheehan, George. *Personal Best*. Emmaus: Rodale Press, 1989.

BIBLIOGRAPHY

Stevens, John. *Budo Secrets*. Boston: Shambhala, 2001.

Suino, Nicklaus. *Arts of Strength, Arts of Serenity*. New York: Weatherhill, 1996.

Sudo, Phillip Toshio. *Zen Guitar*. New York: Simon and Schuster, 1997.

Swados, Elizabeth. *Listening Out Loud*. New York: Harper Row, 1988.

Tanahashi, Kazuaki and Tensho David Schneider. *Essential Zen*. San Francisco: Harper Collins, 1994.

Tanahashi, Kazuaki. *Brush Mind*. Berkeley: Parallax Press, 1990.

Tsunetomo, Yamamoto. *The Book Of Samurai Hagakure*. Tokyo: Kodansha International, 1979.

Ungerleider, Steven. *Mental Training For Peak Performance*. Emmaus: Rodale Press, 1996.

Walker, Brian Brown. *The I Ching*. New York: St. Martin's Griffin, 1992.

Webster-Doyle, Terrence. *Karate: The Art of Empty Self*. Middlebury: Atrium Publications, 1989.

van de Wetering, Janwillem. *The Empty Mirror*. New York: Washington Square Press, 1973.

Wooden, John R. and Steve Jamison. *Wooden*. New York: McGraw-Hill, 1997.

Zinn, Jon Kabat. *Wherever You Go There You Are*. New York: Hyperion, 1994.

Other Works by Jon Hazilla

Recordings as a leader, co-leader *

Chicplacity
The Bitten Moon
C. J. Q. *
Saxabone
Tiny Capers
It Never Entered My Mind
Kaleidoscope *

Book

Mastering The Art Of Brushes

DVD

Brush Control

Credits

Sumi-e Brush Painting on Front Cover:
"Zen Drums" by Jon Hazilla

Photo on Back Cover:
"Buddha Rock Sculpture" by Jon Hazilla

Contact Information

JHazilla@Berklee.edu